John Addington Symonds

In The Key Of Blue

And Other Prose Essays

John Addington Symonds

In The Key Of Blue
And Other Prose Essays

ISBN/EAN: 9783742813589

Manufactured in Europe, USA, Canada, Australia, Japa

Cover: Foto ©Andreas Hilbeck / pixelio.de

Manufactured and distributed by brebook publishing software (www.brebook.com)

John Addington Symonds

In The Key Of Blue

IN THE KEY OF BLUE AND OTHER PROSE ESSAYS BY JOHN ADDINGTON SYMONDS

LONDON ELKIN MATHEWS & JOHN LANE
VIGO STREET
NEW YORK MACMILLAN & COMPANY
MDCCCXCIII

PREFACE

SEVERAL of these Essays have not yet appeared in print. Others are republished from the "Fortnightly," "Contemporary," and "New" Reviews; one from the "Century Guild Hobby-Horse."

There is an interval of more than thirty years between the earliest of the series, "Clifton and a Lad's Love," and the latest.

I have tried to make the selection representative of the different kinds of work in which I have been principally engaged—Greek and Renaissance Literature, Description of Places, Translation, Criticism, Original Verse.

JOHN ADDINGTON SYMONDS.

September 1892.

CONTENTS

	PAGE
THE KEY OF BLUE	1
AMONG THE EUGANEAN HILLS	17
ON AN ALTAR-PIECE BY TIEPOLO	43
THE DANTESQUE AND PLATONIC IDEALS OF LOVE	55
EDWARD CRACROFT LEFROY	87
LA BÊTE HUMAINE	111
MEDIÆVAL NORMAN SONGS	133
CLIFTON AND A LAD'S LOVE	155
NOTES OF A SOMERSETSHIRE HOME	177
CULTURE: ITS MEANING AND ITS USES	195
SOME NOTES ON FLETCHER'S "VALENTINIAN"	217
THE LYRISM OF THE ROMANTIC DRAMA	241
LYRICS FROM ELIZABETHAN SONG-BOOKS	265

IN THE KEY OF BLUE

I

THE nomenclature of colour in literature has always puzzled me. It is easy to talk of green, blue, yellow, red. But when we seek to distinguish the tints of these hues, and to accentuate the special *timbre* of each, we are practically left to suggestions founded upon metaphor and analogy. We select some object in nature—a gem, a flower, an aspect of the sky or sea—which possesses the particular quality we wish to indicate. We talk of grass-green, apple-green, olive-green, emerald-green, sage-green, jade-green; of sapphire, forget-me-not, turquoise, gentian, ultramarine, sky-blue; of topaz, gold, orange, citron; of rose and cherry, ruby and almandine, blood and flame. Or else we use the names of substances from which the pigments are compounded: as yellow-ochre, burnt-sienna, cadmium, lamp-black, verdigris, vermilion, madder, cinnabar. To indicate very subtle gradations, the jargon of commerce supplies us liberally with terms like mauve, magenta, eau-de-Nile, peacock, merda-d'oca, Prussian-blue, crushed strawberry, Venetian-red, gris-de-perle, and so forth to infinity. It is obvious that for purely literary purposes these designations have a very unequal value. Some of them are inadmissible in serious composition. The most precise often fail by interpreting what is absent from the reader's mental eye through what is unknown to his intelligence. Not everybody is familiar with jade, cadmium, almandine, Nile-water. What the writer wants would be a variety of broad terms to express the species (tints) of each genus (hue). In such terms some of the colours are richer than others. Green, I think, is the poorest of all. After verdant, it has to be contented with compounds of itself, like pea-green and those which I have cited above. The Greeks had no generic name for green except one which also meant pale. Next to this they used an adjective derived from the leek. Blue fares better with its azure, cerulean, celestial, amethystine. Yellow is still more fortunate, rejoicing in golden, saffron, orange, flaxen, tawny, blonde. Red stands at the head of the list, possessing a copious vocabulary of ruddy, rosy, russet, crimson, scarlet, pink, sanguine, mulberry, carnation, blushing.

It will be noticed that all these words denominating tints are eventually derived from substances which have been accepted into common parlance. In one shape or another, for example, blood and the rose contribute largely to the phraseology of red.

The poverty of language upon which I am insisting is not wholly disadvantageous to a stylist. It forces him to exercise both fancy and imagination in the effort to bring some special tint before the mental vision of the reader; while all the branches of knowledge at his command, even heraldry, are laid under contribution in turns.

These thoughts were in my mind at Venice, where the problem of colour gradations under their most subtle aspect presents itself on all sides to the artist. I had been especially attracted to the qualities of blue in the dresses of both men and women, and to the behaviour of this colour under various effects of natural and artificial light. Justice has lately been done by some contemporary painters to blue as worn by the Venetian women. But no one, so far as I am aware, has set himself the task of reproducing the costumes of men in single figures or in masses. Yet it is just among the working people—fishermen, stevedores, porters, boatmen, artizans, *facchini*—that the best opportunities are offered for attempting symphonies and harmonies of blue. Whole classes of the male population attire themselves in blouses, sashes, and trousers of this colour. According to the fancy of the individual, or the limitations of his wardrobe, the arrangements of tints are infinitely varied in the same costume. Stuffs faded by washing and exposure blend with new crude dyes. Dirt and stains of labour, patchings of harder upon softer tones, add picturesqueness. And whether the flesh-tints of the man be pale or sun-burned, his complexion dark or fair, blue is equally in sympathy with the model. Some men show remarkable taste in the choice and arrangement of the tints combined. It is clear that they give no little thought to the matter. Modulations from the main chord of three decided blues are made by tones of lavender or mauve in the blouse, the sash, or the stockings. Under strong sunlight, against the greenish water of the canals, the colour effects of such chromatic deviations are piquant and agreeable.

It struck me that it would be amusing to try the resources of our language in a series of studies of what might be termed "blues and blouses." For this purpose I resolved to take a single figure—a *facchino* with whom I have been long acquainted—and to pose him in a variety of lights with a variety of hues in combination.

What follows are notes taken for these studies, most of them, I may add, caught by accident, not sought deliberately.

II

It was a hot June night. Scirocco lay heavy on the air, swathing Venice in damp mists of inky darkness, brooding low upon the city, yet not interfering with the local pungency of lamplight. I had gone with friends to a theatre where Boito's *Mefistofile* was being creditably represented. At the end of the prologue I left the house, intending to return for the prison scene and the beautiful last act. I crossed the Rialto, strolled through the Pescheria, and walked slowly along the Riva dell' Olio. At the very end, upon the barriers of the *traghetto*, under the flaring gas-lamp, Augusto was sitting gazing dreamily and tired across the Grand Canal. Scattered lights broke the surface of the water, and gondolas, like glow-worms, now and then moved silently upon that oily calm. Augusto was intensely blue, giving the single blot of colour on a ground of gloom. This suggested the first of my studies:

A symphony of black and blue—
Venice asleep, vast night, and you.

> *The skies were blurred with vapours dank :*
> *The long canal stretched inky-blank,*
> *With lights on heaving water shed*
> *From lamps that trembled overhead.*
> *Pitch-dark! You were the one thing blue ;*
> *Four tints of pure celestial hue :*
> *The larkspur blouse by tones degraded*
> *Through silken sash of sapphire faded,*
> *The faintly floating violet tie,*
> *The hose of lapis-lazuli.*
> *How blue you were amid that black,*
> *Lighting the wave, the ebon wrack !*
> *The ivory pallor of your face*
> *Gleamed from those glowing azures back*
> *Against the golden gaslight; grapes*
> *Of dusky curls your brows embrace,*
> *And round you all the vast night gapes.*

Augusto, though he was then nineteen years of age, had never left Venice for a day. He once went to Mestre with wine-casks, touched the land, and returned in one of those great *barche*. He wanted to know what the world of fields and woods was like, where horses moved the vehicles, instead of men, and the high-roads are not paved with water. Willing to pleasure him, I proposed that we should spend a couple of days in the Euganean Hills. The first day took us to Val San Zibio. Here we visited that ancient garden of enchantment, with its pleached alleys and labyrinths of box, the gush of mountain streams conducted through stone basins among sculptured deities, the huge umbrageous chestnuts swaying heavy limbs above smooth gravelled paths. We slept at Val San Zibio, in company with silkworms. Next day we drove through Praglia, and round by Rovolone, up to Teolo. On that drive Augusto gave me the second of my studies. His blue dress was now combined with white:

> *A symphony of blues and white—*
> *You, the acacias, dewy-bright,*
> *Transparent skies of chrysolite.*
> *We wind along these leafy hills;*
> *One chord of blue the landscape thrills,*
> *Your three blent azures merged in those*
> *Cerulean heavens above the blouse.*
> *The highest tones flash forth in white:*
> *Acacia branches bowed with snow*
> *Of scented blossom; broken light;*
> *The ivory of your brows, the glow*
> *Of those large orbs that are your eyes:*
> *Those starry orbs of lustrous jet*
> *In clear enamelled turquoise set,*
> *Pale as the marge of morning skies.*

There is an *osteria* in the Calle del Campanile, where I sometimes go to dine with Augusto. The padrona cooks excellently, and the place is frequented by sober people of the quarter. They are all of them very poor, tired with labour, clothed in the most homely garb. At the end of the day's work a little suffices to amuse them—itinerant musicians, a bit of dancing among themselves, a glass of wine added to the frugal store of bread and sausages they bring in handkerchiefs or newspapers. The company is well-bred, and they do not receive a stranger unwillingly, provided they see that he has found a mate of their own kindred. It was here that Augusto suggested the third of my studies in blue:

> *A symphony of blues and brown—*
> *We were together in the town:*
> *A grimy tavern with blurred walls,*
> *Where dingy lamplight floats and falls*
> *On working men and women, clad*
> *In sober watchet, umber sad.*
> *Two viols and one 'cello scream*
> *Waltz music through the smoke and steam:*
> *You rise, you clasp a comrade, who*
> *Is clothed in triple blues like you:*
> *Sunk in some dream voluptuously*
> *Circle those azures richly blent,*
> *Swim through the dusk, the melody;*
> *Languidly breathing, you and he,*
> *Uplifting the environment;*
> *Ivory face and swart face laid*
> *Cheek unto cheek, like man, like maid.*

The host of this *osteria*, which has no name or sign by which it may be known, is called Giovanni. The blank back of the Church of S. Casciano frowns down upon his house, and chokes the light out. He has a heap of children, the youngest of whom come home at nightfall just after we have finished supper. Augusto one evening took a little bright-eyed girl belonging to the family upon his knee. We were sitting with the table between us, and a gas lamp above our heads. That is the *motif* of my fourth study:

> A symphony of pink and blue,
> The lamp, the little maid, and you.
> Your strong man's stature in those three
> Blent azures clothed, so loved by me;
> Your grave face framed in felt thrown back;
> Your sad sweet lips, eyes glossy black,
> Now laughing, while your wan cheeks flush
> Like warm white roses with a blush.
> Clasped to your breast, held by your hands,
> Smothered in blues, the baby stands:
> Her frock like some carnation gleams;
> Her hair, a golden torrent, streams:
> Blue as forget-me-not her eyes,
> Or azure-wingèd butterflies:
> Her cheeks and mouth so richly red,
> One would not think her city-bred.
> Your beautiful pale face of pain
> Leaned to the child's cheeks breathing health;
> Like feathers dropped from raven's wing,
> The curls that round your forehead rain
> Merged with her tresses' yellowy wealth;
> Her mouth that was a rose in spring

> Touched yours, her pouting nether lip
> Clasped your fine upper lip, whose brink,
> Wherefrom Love's self a bee might sip,
> Is pencilled with faint Indian ink.
> Such was the group I saw one night
> Illumined by a flaring light,
> In that dim tavern where we meet
> Sometimes to smoke, and drink and eat;
> Exquisite contrast, not of tone,
> Or tint, or form, or face alone.

Augusto and I were once more in the country together. This time we fared further, and found a nook of the hills which was all overgrown with yellow shrubs and plants in bloom. The sunlight was intense, and summer in the air. He lay prone in grass, which was not so much grass as a vast field of cloth of gold. The blues he wore struck me as giving its accent to the scene, and so I made a fifth study:

> A symphony of blues and gold,
> Among ravines of grey stones rolled
> Adown the steep from mountains old.
> Laburnum branches drop their dew
> Of amber bloom on me, on you:
> With cytisus and paler broom,
> Electron glimmering through the gloom.
> Around us all the field flames up,
> Goldenrod, hawkweed, buttercup;
> While curling through lush grass one spies
> Tendrils of honeyed helichryse.

> *'Tis saffron, topaz, solar rays,*
> *Dissolved in fervent chrysoprase.*
> *Cool, yet how luminous, the blue,*
> *Centred in triple tones by you,*
> *Uniting all that yellow glare*
> *With the blue circumambient air,*
> *The violet shades, the hard cobalt*
> *Of noon's inexorable vault.*

How are blues to be combined with green? That question haunted me, until I passed in my gondola one day down a narrow Rio, where there was a dyer's workshop. Augusto had nothing to do with the study which I place sixth on my list. It must be noticed that the tone of blue here indicated is very low, and that of green is diminished to mere notes and suggestions. It might have been possible to discover a concord of blue and green under intenser conditions of light and colour, as when, in the afterglow, barges laden with fresh-cut grass glide against the purples of the east. Yet, as I saw the harmony, I give it here in verse:

> *A symphony of blues and green,*
> *Swart indigo and eau-marine.*
> *Stripped to the waist two dyers kneel*
> *On grey steps strewn with orange peel;*
> *The glaucous water to the brink*
> *Welters with clouds of purplish ink:*
> *The men wring cloth that drips and takes*
> *Verditer hues of water-snakes,*

*While pali paled by sun and seas
Repeat the tint in verdigris.
Those brows, nude breasts, and arms of might,
The pride of youth and manhood white,
Now smirched with woad, proclaim the doom
Of labour and its life-long gloom.
Only the eyes emergent shine,
These black as coals, those opaline;
Lighten from storms of tangled hair,
Black curls and blonde curls debonnair,
Proving man's untamed spirit there.*

The lagoon toward Fusina takes the whole glory of Venetian sunset. The sun sinks down into the Lombard plain, incarnadining the vault of clouds and the vast mirrors of the undulating water floor. Colours which are cold by nature now assume an unexpected warmth. The blue of blouse and sash and trousers passes transfigured into gems or flowers. It is raised to amethyst, irradiated with crimson. Alone with Augusto at such a moment, I obtained the seventh of my studies:

*A symphony of blues and red—
The broad lagoon, and overhead
Sunset, a sanguine banner, spread.
Fretty of azure and pure gules
Are sea, sky, city, stagnant pools:
You, by my side, within the boat,
Imperially purple float,
Beneath a burning sail, straight on
Into the west's vermilion.*

IN THE KEY OF BLUE

The triple azures melt and glow
Like flaunting iris-flowers arow;
One amethystine gem of three
Fused by the heaven's effulgency.
Now fails the splendour, day dies down
Beyond the hills by Padua's town;
And all along the eastern sky
Blue reassumes ascendency.
Lapped in those tints of fluor-spar,
You shine intense, an azure star,
With roses flushed that slowly fade
Against the vast aërial shade.

I have made Augusto pose long enough as a mere model or lay figure, dressed in three sorts of blue, composing pictures. The next study, in which the sense of colour is not wholly lost, deals at last with more actual and kindly human sympathies. I give it as the record of a day spent in a little town between Treviso and Vicenza. The old towers and walls of Castelfranco still exist; and a moat surrounds them filled with running water. The walls and turrets rise, covered here and there with ivy, from green banks—intensely red in their time-mellowed brickwork. The banks are planted like a garden with flowering shrubs and trees, among which, at the time of our visit, clumps of Guelder roses, with their heavy white bosses in full bloom, were conspicuous. Around the ancient burgh, separated from the moat by a broad high-road, runs a suburb of low houses, with mediæval arcades; and there are avenues of tall white poplars. The town and its suburb form two squares, at one angle of which, fronting Giorgione's great white marble statue, is the Albergo della Spada, a Venetian palace with Gothic windows, and a balustraded balcony adorned with little seated lions.

> *At Castelfranco, with a blouse*
> *Venetian, blent of triple blues,*
> *I walked all through the sleepy town,*
> *Worshipped Madonna gazing down*
> *From that high throne Giorgione painted*
> *Above the knight and friar sainted,*
> *Drank in the landscape golden-green,*
> *The dim primeval pastoral scene.*
> *The blouse beside me thrilled no less*
> *Than I to that mute loveliness;*
> *Spoke little, turned aside, and dwelt*
> *Perchance on what he dumbly felt.*
> *There throbbed a man's heart neath the shirt,*
> *The sash, the hose, a life alert,*
> *Veiled by that dominating hurt.*
> *Then swept a storm-cloud from the hills;*
> *Eddying dust the city fills,*
> *The thunder crashes, and the rain*
> *Hisses on roof and flooded plain.*
> *Ere midnight, when the moon sailed low,*
> *Peering through veils of indigo,*
> *We went abroad, and heard the wail*
> *Of many a darkling nightingale,*

IN THE KEY OF BLUE

Pouring as birds will only pour
Their souls forth when heaven's strife is o'er.
Those red walls, and the mighty towers,
Which lustrous ivy over-flowers,
Loomed through the murk divinely warm,
As palpitating after storm.
Hushed was the night for friendly talk;
Under the dark arcades we walk,
Pace the wet pavement, where light steals
And swoons amid the huge abeles:
Then seek our chamber. All the blues
Dissolve, the symphony of hues
Fades out of sight, and leaves at length
A flawless form of simple strength,
Sleep-seeking, breathing, ivory-white,
Upon the couch in candle-light.

I will now close this fantasia on blues and blouses with an envoy to the man who helped to make it. An artist in language must feel the mockery of word-painting, though he is often seduced to attempt effects which can only be adequately rendered by the palette. Description is not the proper end of writing. Word-paintings are a kind of hybrid, and purists in art criticism not irrationally look askance at the mixed species.

"Pictures or poems? Dithyramb or prose?
What are they?" cries this critic. This replies:
"Word-pictures or verse-idylls, no man knows!"
"One thing is sure," a third saith: "Sure he lies,
Who finds in these thrice-sifted rhapsodies

> *The stuff of good plain writing!" "Put them by,"*
> *A fourth, more cautious, murmurs; "time will try."*
>
> *Were silence, then, not better than this speech?*
> *Words do no work of pencil, palette, brush,*
> *Words are designed to thrill the heart, or teach;*
> *Not to depict, not to revoke the blush*
> *Of dawn, or reincarnadine the flush*
> *Of sunset; break this wavering wand, and go*
> *Back to thy books, poor powerless Prospero.*

Nevertheless, something may still be pleaded in favour of verbal description. If it be sufficiently penetrated with emotion, it has by its very vagueness a power of suggestion which the more direct art of the painter often misses. Sympathetic minds are stimulated to acts of creation by the writer, while pictures make demands upon their assimilative faculties alone.

> *How can words paint this warmth of blues,*
> *Blended with black, white, brown, all hues?*
> *Longhi we want, Tiepolo,*
> *To make us moderns feel blue so:*
> *They knew the deep Venetian night,*
> *The values of Venetian light,*
> *Venetian blouses led them right.*
> *Come back, my Muse, come back to him*
> *Who warmed the cold hue, bright or dim.*
> *Those ivory brows, those lustrous eyes,*
> *Those grape-like curls, those brief replies;*
> *These are thy themes—the man, the life—*
> *Not tints in symphony at strife.*

AMONG THE EUGANEAN HILLS

I

A LAND less rich in natural, artistic, and historical attractions than Italy could not afford to leave a district so charming as that of the Euganean Hills almost unknown, unvisited. No guide-books talk about these little mountains; there is nothing of importance, so far as I am aware, written on them from the historical or any other point of view. Express trains carry troops of tourists along their outskirts from Bologna to Padua and *vice versâ*. All English people who read our poets know that Shelley called them—

> "*Those famous Euganean hills which bear,
> As seen from Lido through the harbour piles,
> The likeness of a clump of peakèd isles.*"

Their purple pyramids, lifted against the orange of the western sky, form an indispensable ingredient of the orthodox Venetian sunset. Their reflections in the blue mirror of the lagoons, although they are so far away, count as one of the chief wonders of the beautiful Venetian mornings. Yet I rarely meet with man or woman who has had the curiosity to invade the Oreads of the Euganeans in their native haunts, and to pluck the heart out of their poetic mystery.

It has been my own good fortune to spend several weeks on different occasions at the villa of a noble lady who resides not far from Monselice. So I have enjoyed special opportunities of becoming acquainted with this fascinating island in the ocean of the Lombard plain. For variety and delicacy of detail, for miniature mountain grandeur, it may be compared with what we call the English Lakes. The scale is nearly similar, though the Euganeans are positively smaller, and are placed in far more interesting surroundings. What they lack is water. This defect is balanced by the richness of Italian vegetation, by the breadth of the great landscape out of which they heave, by the immediate neighbourhood of famous cities, and by the range of snowy Alps which tower upon their northern horizon.

I cannot offer anything like a detailed study of the Euganean Hills. What follows in

AMONG THE EUGANEAN HILLS

these pages consists of three extracts from my diary, made in the May month of three several years, relating aimless but highly enjoyable ramblings about their gentle declivities and wooded valleys.

II

Este is a town of great antiquity, mentioned under its old name of Ateste both by Tacitus and Pliny. The Adige in former times flowed by its walls; and etymologists derive the city's name from Athesis. The museum is rich in Roman inscriptions, which are said to have drawn Professor Mommsen on a visit to the quiet place. Here in the Middle Ages dwelt the Italian members of the mighty house of Guelph; who took their title from Este, and afterwards ruled Ferrara, Modena, and Reggio as Dukes. At present the town has little to show of interest, except some picturesque ruins of wall and tower, crumbling away upon the southern promontory of the Euganeans, under slopes of olive and almond and vine.

Just above the town, surveying it from a kind of terrace, is the villa called I Cappuccini, which Lord Byron lent to the Shelleys in the autumn of 1818. "We have been living," writes Shelley to Peacock on the 8th of October, "this last month near the little town from which I date this letter, in a very pleasant villa which has been lent to us. Behind here are the Euganean hills, not so beautiful as those of the Bagni di Lucca, with Arquá, where Petrarch's house and tomb are religiously preserved and visited. At the end of our garden is an extensive Gothic castle, now the habitation of owls and bats, where the Medici family resided before they came to Florence. We see before us the wide, flat plain of Lombardy, in which we see the sun and moon rise and set, and the evening star, and all the golden magnificence of autumnal clouds." I do not know to what tradition about the Medici Shelley was referring. It is true that Cosmo di Medici was banished in 1433 to Padua; and he may possibly have spent part of his short exile at Este. I think it more probable, however, that Shelley confused the Medici with the Dukes of Ferrara, who took their family title from the old fief of Este.

In this villa Shelley composed the first part of *Prometheus Unbound*. "I have been writing, and indeed have just finished, the first act of a lyric and classical drama, to be called *Prometheus Unbound*." From Padua he wrote, September 22, to his "best Mary": "Bring the sheets of *Prometheus Unbound*, which you will find numbered from 1 to 26 on the table of the pavilion." The people who now inhabit I Cappuccini still show this pavilion, a little dilapidated summer-house, overgrown with ivy, at the end of a garden terrace. It was also near Este, having climbed one of the many-peaked summits above the town, that Shelley improvised the "Lines written in the Euganean Hills."

From Este to Arquá is no great distance. The road for some time skirts the hills, then turns abruptly upward to the left, leading to the village, which is picturesquely placed among its fruit-trees in a hollow of the arid limestone mountains. Arquá looks at first sight like a tiny piece of the Riviera, with the hazy Lombard plain in lieu of the Mediterranean. Petrarch's house is a fair-sized white cottage at the extreme end of the village, one of the highest dwellings of Arquá. From its windows and garden-walls the eye ranges across olive-trees, laurels, and pomegranates to the misty level land which melts into the sea; churches with their companili rising from the undetermined azure, like great galleys stranded in a lagoon. It is the constant recurrence of this Lombard distance, the doubt whether we are gazing upon land or sea, the sense of the neighbouring Adriatic and Venetian salt-lakes, which lends a peculiar charm to Euganean landscapes.

Petrarch's study is a tiny room, with a little northern window, opening out of a larger antechamber. There was just enough space in it to hold a table and his arm-chair, which is still preserved, as well as a book-cupboard. Here, then, the old poet fell asleep for the last time among his books, upon the 18th of June 1374. He had lived at Arquá since 1369, studying incessantly and writing with assiduity till the very end. One of the last things he composed was a Latin version of his friend Boccaccio's story of Griselda. They show the mummy of a cat, wholly destitute of hair, which is said to have once been his " furry favourite." Probably the beast is no more genuine than Wallenstein's celebrated horse at Prague.

The house contains several spacious rooms, with chimney-pieces of a later date, and frescoes setting forth in quaint *quattrocento* style the loves of Laura and the poet. One of these, which represents the meeting of Petrarch and his lady, might almost be called pretty; a bushy laurel sprouts from Petrarch's head, Laura has a Cupid near her; both are pacing in a verdant meadow.

The village church of Arquá stands upon an open terrace with a full stream of clearest water —*chiare e fresche onde*—flowing by. On the square before its portal, where the peasants congregate at mass-time, rises the tomb of

Petrarch: a simple rectilinear coffin of smooth Verona marble, raised on four thick columns, and covered with a pyramidal lid—what the Italians call an *arca*. Without emblems, allegories, or lamenting genii, this tomb of the inspired poet, the acute student who opened a new age of intellectual activity for Europe, suggests thoughts beyond the reach of words. Petrarch was emphatically the first modern man, the individuality who began to disengage art and letters from mediævalism. Here he sleeps, encircled by the hills, beneath the canopy of heaven; and his own winged thoughts, "forms more real than living man, nurslings of immortality," the ethereal offspring of his restless heart and brain, seem to keep watch around him in the liquid air.

There is a village inn within a few steps of this piazza, where the excellent white wine of Arquá may be tasted with advantage. Grown upon that warm volcanic soil of the Euganeans, in the pure dry climate of the hills, it is generous and light together. Experience leads me to believe that it does not bear transportation; for the Arquà wine one sometimes finds in Venice has lost in quality. This, however, is a characteristic of very many Italian wines; and nothing is more charming in that incomparable country than the surprises which are always awaiting the œnophilist (as Thackeray calls him) in unexpected places, villages unknown to fame, and wayside hostelries.

To Battaglia we drive through a swamp of willows and tall bullrushes and bending reeds. The quiet pools and dykes which slumber in this mass of vegetation are abloom with white and yellow water-lilies, iris, water-violet, and flowering rush. Some great birds—wild geese, I think—were flying and feeding there, as I drove through the marshland in the early morning.

Battaglia and the neighbouring village of Abano are both celebrated for their baths and springs of hot sulphurous water. Here we understand in how true a sense the Euganean Hills are a volcanic upheaval from what must have been a great sea at the time of their emergence. The ground is so hot and hollow, so crusted with salts and crystalline deposits, and the water which spouts up in miniature geysers is so boiling, that one wonders when a new eruption is going to take place. On autumn evenings, a mist from the warm springs hangs over Abano, giving it a dreamy look as the train whisks by. But this is no vapour of malaria. The country indeed is singularly healthy. Abano was known to the Romans. They called it Aponus ; the name being derived, it is said, from a Greek adjective which means *painless*—a kind of parallel to Posilippo. Hundreds of folk, then as now, came to rid themselves of rheumatic pains and other ailments in the mud-baths and hot mineral water. Suetonius says that when Tiberius was a young man, the object of suspicion to his stepfather, Augustus, he visited Padua upon the occasion of a journey into Illyria. "There he consulted the oracle of Geryon, which bade him cast golden dice into the fountain of Aponus, in order to obtain an answer to his questions. This he did accordingly, and the dice thrown by him turned up the highest possible numbers. The dice themselves can be seen to this day in the water."

Geryon, according to one version of his legend, was a king of Hesperia ; and Hercules is said to have opened the springs of Battaglia and Abano by ploughing with his oxen there. The ancients seem to have symbolised the volcanic nature of this country in several myths. It is difficult not to connect the legend of Phaethon, who fell from heaven into the Po, burned up the waters of Eridanus, and converted the tears of the river-nymphs to amber, with some dim memory of primitive convulsions. At this point I would fain turn aside to dally with the two books of Pontano's *Eridani*, than which modern scholarship has produced nothing more liquid, more poetical, more original in Latin verse. But *ne quid nimis:* for now the domes and towers of Padua begin to loom in the distance—the vast roof of the Palazzo Ragione, the fanciful cupolas of S. Antonio, harmonious and lovely S. Giustina—while we jog along the never-ending straight banks of the canal, and the Euganeans sink cloudlike into azure air behind us.

III

Two days ago I started with three friends, two Venetians and an Englishman, for the Euganean Hills. The day was very hot for the season, since we are still in the middle of May. Our object was to make an early ascent of Venda, the highest point of the group, which looks so graceful and so lofty from the lagoons near Malamocco. Venda rises only a little over two thousand feet above the sea. But it has the sweep and outline of a grand mountain.

We spent the afternoon and evening at Val San Zibio, in the Albergo alla Pergola: about half an hour's drive out of Battaglia. There is a villa there with gardens, built and planned originally in the early seventeenth century by a member of the Barbarigo family. The place afterwards passed to the Martinenghi of Venice, and now belongs to the Conte Donà delle Rose.

The dwelling-house has been modernised and ruined in appearance by the destruction of the statues and florid architectural decorations which brought it formerly into keeping with those massive walls, old-fashioned iron gratings, barocco groups of gods on balustrades and fountains, remaining in the ancient pleasure-ground. On the great front gates to the garden, where the water from the hills comes rushing down by steps, the coat of Barbarigo is splendidly displayed: "*Argent* on a bend *gules*, between six beards *sable*, three lioncels passant *or.*" It is the same coat which adorns the Scala dei Giganti and one of the great chimney-pieces in the Ducal Palace.

There is nothing, perhaps, exactly comparable to this old-world garden at Val San Zibio. Placed at the opening of a little glen, or coomb, descending from a spur of Venda, it fills the whole space up, and works into complete harmony with the surrounding wildness. The formal landscape gardening of two centuries ago has been mellowed by time, so as to merge imperceptibly, without the slightest break or discord, into bowery woods and swelling hills. The compassed fish-ponds, the moss-grown statues of aquatic deities, the Cupids holding dolphins which spout threads of water from their throats, the labyrinth of clipped box, the huge horse-chestnut trees, the long green alleys of hornbeam twisted into ogee arches overhead, the smooth-shaven lawns, and the myriad gold-fish in the water-lilied tanks—all these elements of an aristocratic pleasance melt, as it were, into the gentle serenity of the leafy heights above them, the solemnity of cypress avenues, the hoary stillness of olive orchards, the copses of hazel, elm, acacia, chestnut. Nowhere, indeed, have I seen art and nature married by time and taste with such propriety and sympathy of feeling. It is delightful to saunter through those peaceful walks, to hear the gush of waterfalls, and to watch the fountains play, while the sun is westering, and the golden-verdant cup of the little valley swims in light-irradiated haze.

We four friends enjoyed this pastime for an hour or so; and then, after strolling awhile in acacia woods above the hamlet, we returned to an excellent supper at our inn. It was served in a corner of the kitchen: one of those large brick-floored rooms, with wooden rafters, and a pent-house chimney-piece half open to the air, which Tintoretto sometimes painted—notably in his Cenacolo, at the Scuola di S. Rocco. Such kitchens always contain an abundance of copper vessels and brass salvers hung about the walls, from the appearance of which the wary guest may form a tolerably accurate prognostication of his coming meal. At our hostel of the Pergola the copper and brass gear was not only plentiful, but almost as dazzling as Atlante's shield in the *Orlando*. And the supper corresponded to these happy auspices. Signora Fortin, our hostess, served it with her own hands, hissing from the hearth. The *menu* ran as follows:—"Risi-bisi," a Venetian mess of rice and young peas stewed in gravy; veal cutlets, with asparagus; lettuce-salad, home-made sausage, and cheese from the pastures. Good white wine of the Arquà type satisfied our thirst; and when the simple meal was finished, my three companions sat down to play *tresètt* with the jovial Boniface. I, who had no skill at cards, wandered out into the moonlight, pacing country lanes alive with fire-flies and glow-worms. Then came the divine night of sleep in lowly bed-chambers with open windows, through which entered the songs of nightingales, the plash of falling waters, and the sough of heavy-foliaged trees.

In the morning we started at six o'clock for Venda. We had been promised a *putelo*, a *ragazzo*—a boy, in fact, to carry our provisions. He turned out a red-haired toper, over fifty years of age, with a fiery nose. However, he performed his function as a beast of burden. The hedgerows were drenched with dew, bringing out the scent of wild-rose, privet, and acacia-blossom. Scirocco brooded in the air, foreboding an afternoon of thunderstorm. From Galzignano, a village at the foot of our mountain, we began the ascent to Rua—the first stage of the easy climb. The hillsides here were abloom with silver cistus, golden broom, gaudy orchises, starred anthericum lilies, purple columbines, and creamy potentillas swaying from a slender stalk. Rua is a spacious convent, covering several acres on a spur of Venda. Within its walled enclosure are separate dwellings for the monks who live there, cottages united by common allegiance to the church which rises in their midst. It ought to be a paradise for men who have renounced the world, desire seclusion, and are contented with a round of rustic labour and religious duties. But as we skirted the long wall of the convent precincts, I wondered how many of its inmates may have missed their vocation—for whom that vast extent of landscape and the distant cities seen upon the plain are only sources of perpetual irritation. For, as we rose, the view expanded; the isolated position of the Euganeans, like an island in an immense sea, made itself more and more felt. By glimpses through the thickets of dwarf chestnut, hornbeam, or hazel, we gazed upon aërial Alps, long silvery lagoons, the lapse of rivers flowing to the Adriatic, and brown villages with bell-towers for their centre.

The summit of Venda is a long rolling down, which reminded me of the Feldberg in the Black

Forest. The ruins of an ancient convent crown its southern crest. This must have erewhile been a noble edifice; for the abandoned walls are built to last for ever, in a severely massive Benedictine style. They abut upon a kind of precipice; and the prospect they command is the whole Lombard plain to south and west, fringed with the silver-edged lagoons and sea, threaded by the Adige, and gemmed with venerable seats of human habitation, among which Montagnana stands conspicuous. Upon the other side of Venda, the line of the Tyrolese and Friulian Alps breaks the northern sky; Brenta flows through the fields to Padua; and the Monti Berici, descending from the mountains of Vicenza, stretch out their feelers till they almost touch the Euganeans at Bastia. From this point, as from the top of one of those raised maps men make in Switzerland, we can study the structure of the tiny group of mountains Venda crowns—so small in scale, so exquisitely modelled, so finely pencilled in its valley structure, so rich in human life and vegetation.

It would be impossible to spend some hours upon the crest of Venda, and not to think of Shelley's poem. As a boy, I had those lines by heart, and used to wonder dreamily about the memorable landscape they describe:

> "*Beneath is spread like a green sea
> The waveless plain of Lombardy,
> Bounded by the vapourous air,
> Islanded by cities fair;
> Underneath day's azure eyes
> Ocean's nursling, Venice lies,
> A peopled labyrinth of walls,
> Amphitrite's destined halls.*"

How true the picture is! And then again:

> "*By the skirts of that grey cloud
> Many-doméd Padua proud
> Stands, a peopled solitude,
> 'Mid the harvest-shining plain,
> Where the peasant heaps his grain.*"

Yes, indeed, there is Venice, there is Padua, there are the skirts of the grey cloud; but the Celtic anarch, the foes, the tyrants, of whom Shelley sang, have now disappeared from Italy. Are her sons happier, I asked myself, than when the Frenchmen and the Austrians were here?

While I was making these reflections, there appeared upon the scene a youthful cowherd, or *vacher*, with a hungry hound who loved him. He was a bright lad, clear-cut in feature, nut-brown of complexion, white of teeth, with pale blue wistful eyes. He told us that he could neither read nor write, that his mother was dead, and his father confined in the madhouse of San Servolo. He had been born and bred on Venda; and now he had drawn a number for the army, and was just going to be drafted into some regiment. I gave him my briar pipe for a keepsake; and then, having already spent three lazy hours upon the top of Venda, we began the descent upon the other side, breaking into thickets of low brushwood. Here the air became heavy with an aromatic resinous scent, which I soon perceived to come from the mystic *Dictamnus fraxinella* in full bloom. The coppice reddened far and wide with the tall spires of that remarkably handsome flower. At night, in certain conditions of the weather, it is said to be phosphorescent; or, to put the fact perhaps more accurately, it emits volatile oil in large quantities, which readily ignites and burns with a pale bluish flame around the ruddy blossoms. After following a ridge, partly wooded and partly down-land, for about an hour, we came to the opening of the Val San Zibio ravine. Into this we plunged—into a dense, silent, icy-cold wood of hazels—where the air seemed frozen by contrast with the burning sunlight we had left. The descent through the coomb or gully to the quiet hamlet, deep in verdure, called to mind many a Devonshire or Somersetshire glen.

This morning, on the way back to Venice, I visited Cataio, a castle built in the sixteenth century by one of the Obizzi family. It is a huge place, designed in a fanciful style, half Renaissance palace, half barrack. A broad flight of steps leads to a vast terrace high above the courts and gardens, which commands an enchanting prospect over the plain of Battaglia, the hazy glens and outskirts of the Euganeans, and the cloudlike mass of Venda. Here I bade adieu to the mountain and to the pleasant solitudes of Val San Zibio.

IV

The third extract from my diary shows me again at Val San Zibio, next year, upon the very same day of the month, strolling about the lovely pleasance, this time in different company. It is Sunday morning, and the peasants, both men and women, carry roses stuck behind their ears. One grey-haired old fellow, who is the Conte's bailiff, wore two large China roses, one for each side of his ruddy countenance.

Domenico, the coachman, arrived at eight, and having said farewell to the jolly Boniface of the Pergola, we started on our long day's expedition. Skirting the hills by Galzignano and across the spurs of Venda, we pass through a land of changeful beauty. The whole country is in

AMONG THE EUGANEAN HILLS

bloom upon this glorious summer morning. In none of my wanderings have I seen such torrents of acacia-blossom, whitening acres of the hillside, making the ridges hoary and the glens one snowdrift, lifting plumes of rosy or of creamy silver into the fiery blue of heaven above our eyes. Ruddy-fruited cherry-trees, grey-green olives, glossy chestnuts, with mulberries and figs and peach-trees, all attired in daintiest green, interpenetrate this riot of acacia-blossom; and the air is alive with dragon-flies in thousands, chasing each other through the liquid light. Here and there wild nature asserts her independence. The signs of tilth and culture fade off into tangles of cistus, Mediterranean heath, broom, myrtle, arbutus, and juniper, overflowing from the arid sandstone slopes, just like the *maquis* of Corsica. Then follow orchards of apples, almonds, pears, plums, apricots. Copses of walnuts and chestnuts break into vineyards or pastures bordered with dykes full of yellow iris and nymphea. This variety within a narrow compass, due to the rise and fall of the land, and also to abrupt geological changes, constitutes the chief charm of travelling in the Euganeans.

So, in due course of time, we arrived at the great Benedictine Abbey of Praglia, now used as a barrack, where troops of all descriptions come from time to time on camping expeditions. They bring their bedding and furniture with them, and take it away when they depart ; so that in their absence the interminable corridors and cells, refectories and parlours, cloisters and courts, are whitewashed and dreary, scrawled over with the names and jests of soldiers. Only two Padri are left ; "*Custodi* for the State in a house where we were once *Padroni*," said one of them with a bitter smile, as he pointed to the ruthlessly dilapidated library, the empty bookcases, the yawning framework of the wooden ceiling, whence pictures had been torn. These Padri simply loathe the soldiers.

The architectural interest of Praglia centres in three large cloisters, one of them lifted high in air above magazines, cellars, and storehouses. The refectory, too, is a noble chamber ; and the church is spacious. But the whole building impresses the imagination by magnitude, solidity, severity—true Benedictine qualities—rather than by beauty of form or brilliance of fancy. We find nothing here of the harmonious grace (of what Alberti called *tutta quella musica*, that music of the classic style) which is so conspicuous in S. Giustina at Padua, itself an offshoot from the mighty Abbey. The situation, too, though certainly agreeable, on the skirts of the hills, with a fair prospect over the broad champaign, lacks that poetry of which one finds so much in all parts of the Euganeans. Praglia might be called a good specimen of massive ecclesiastical prose.

We jogged on, through Montemerlo, toward the group of hills which divide Teolo from Rovolone, having the jagged cliffs of Pendice first in sight, and then the deeply wooded Madonna del Monte on our left hand, and the Paduan plain upon the right. After about four miles of this travelling under the noonday sun, the road bends suddenly upwards, striking into wood and coppice. The summit of the little pass affords a double vista; backwards over the illimitable plain with Padua stretched out like a map in hazy sunshine; forwards to Bastia and the Monti Berici. These miniature *cols*, deep in chestnut and acacia groves, with the gracefully shaped crests above them, make one of the main beauties of the Euganeans. Tall purple orchids, splashed with white, began to gleam in the thick grasses, while here and there a flame-like spire of fraxinella-bloom reminded me of Venda.

At length we plunged into the deep woods and country lanes of Rovolone, remarkably English in character, and halted at a roadside *osteria*. The red wine here was excellent—one of those surprises which reward the diligent œnophilist in Italy. I decided to walk up to the church, remembering our autumn visit of 1888, when a dear friend of mine lay and shed tears on the parapet. *E vide e pianse il fato amaro*, for he had to leave Lombardy next day for London and the British Museum. To-day the landscape swam in summer heat, out of which emerged the spurs of the Monti Berici, amethystine-blue ; and the Alpine chain, which was so white and glittering on that October afternoon, could now be hardly detected through sultry vapour. So I retraced my steps down the rough sandstone road, following the tinkling streamlet, between overarching boughs of maple, hornbeam, and wild cherry. I found Domenico and Augusto still drinking the excellent red wine and eating *salame* in the osteria. When the nag was rested, we helped him and the carriage down a broken lane —more torrent-bed than pathway—into the main road to Vo. At this point we struck abruptly upward to the left, and reached Teolo through a long straight valley between limestone hills. The variety of soil, and the sudden alteration from one kind of rock to another in the Euganeans, together with the change of flora this implies, is another of their charms. Here I noticed abundance of tree-heath and starry snow-white anthericum.

At the head of this long valley the view gradually broadens out on every side. Teolo is magnificently situated between the Madonna del Monte and more distant Venda—Venda stretching like a great green cloud, with Rua perched upon its eastern spur, and the ruins of the convent crowning the irregular summit. But between the town and Venda lies a wide expanse of undulating country, out of the verdure of which shoot the grey double crags of Pendice, in form reminding one not very distantly of Langdale Pikes.

Teolo occupies incomparably the finest point, as it also is the central point, of the Euganean district. It is important enough to be a station for Carabinieri. Yet the little township lies so scattered on the hillsides, that in my Alpine home we should call it a *Landschaft*. I thought involuntarily of Cadore, as I stood before the door of the inn, an isolated house, the last house of the village. There is a touch of Dolomite feeling about the scenery of Teolo.

Domenico bade me go to sleep for a couple of hours, which I did as well as I could through the noise and singing of fifteen Venetian *cortesani* in the next room. At six o'clock he called me to begin the ascent of Pendice. Leaving the street behind us, we passed out upon a ridge which joins the terrace-side of Teolo to the larger block of precipice and forest called Pendice. Here one looks both ways over the Lombard plain, spread out literally like an ocean, and framed, as the sea might be framed, by the inverted angles of valleys descending into it on either hand. It took us rather more than half an hour to reach the summit of the rock by a pretty steep footpath. I suppose the crags in vertical height on the eastern side are about two hundred feet above the woods, which fall away steeply to the valley bottom at the distance of some three hundred feet farther. So the impression of altitude is considerable, and the fine bold cleavage of the stone increases the effect. There are extensive and massive remains of what must have once been a very formidable castle, covering the whole of the upper platform, and descending for a certain distance upon either side. Henbane grows in rank luxuriance around these ruins. But I am ashamed to say that I know nothing about the history of this stronghold, nor about Speronella, the mediæval heroine of its romance. An old peasant who lives up there, like an owl in a corner of the ruin, could give no information. He waxed eloquent about monks and bandits, bravi and maidens confined in subterranean grottoes; but of facts he was as ignorant as I am.

From this point of vantage the view is really glorious; so much of plain visible to east and west as gives a sense of illimitable space, without the monotony of one uniform horizon; then the great billowy mass of Venda, the crest of Madonna del Monte, and the rich green labyrinth of dales and copses at one's feet. A furious wind flew over us; and a thunderstorm swept across the southern sky, passing probably between Este and the Adige, lightening and thundering incessantly. The old peasant told us not to be anxious; the storm was not coming our way. So we sat down beneath a broken wall, which seemed to tremble in the blast, and enjoyed the lurid commotion of the heavens, which added sublimity to the landscape. All this while the sun was setting, flaringly red and angry, in crimson contrast with the tawny purples of the tempest clouds. The verdure of hill, wood, and meadow assumed that peculiar brilliancy which can only be compared to chrysoprase; and all the reaches of the Lombard plain smouldered in violet blue. The sun dropped behind the Monti Berici, and we clambered down from our eyrie, glad to regain the inn, to sup and sleep.

I will save one tiny episode from the ascent to Pendice, and put it in the form of a dialogue, as it really happened.

Domenico.—What herb is that?

The Peasant.—Hemlock.

Augusto. (*bending down to touch the plant.*)— Poor Socrates!

I.—Socrates was the Jesus Christ of Greece.
Augusto.—Just so.

Next day, the whim came over me to drive the whole way from Teolo, through Padua, Stra, Dolo, to Mestre, and to regain Venice by the lagoon. It meant rising at four and reaching home at seven. But I wanted to get a notion of what travelling was like in Lombardy before the age of railways.

ON AN ALTAR-PIECE BY TIEPOLO

VENICE in the last century produced four eminent painters, Giovanni Battista Tiepolo, Canaletto, Guardi, Longhi. Of these Tiepolo was by far the greatest, in natural endowment, in splendour of performance, in fecundity of production. Believers in metempsychosis might have sworn, seeing his grand style bud and bloom in that degenerate age, that Paolo Veronese lived again in Tiepolo's body. He has the same sincerity of conception, the same firmness of execution, the same largeness, breadth, serenity and sanity, that we admire in the earlier master. This is felt in the frescoes of the Palazzo Labia, where the loves of Antony and Cleopatra fill immense spaces with mundane pomp and insolent animalism. How grandly the great scenes are planned; how large and luminous the sky-regions, where masts bristle and pennants flutter to the breeze of Cydnus; how noble the orders of the architecture, enclosing groups of men and women, horses, dwarfs, dogs, all in stately movement or superb repose! Then the fresco-painting is so solid, the drawing and design so satisfactory, the colouring so rich and varied, the types and characters in face and form so strongly marked. Of a truth, we say, here is a master of the heroic age come to life once more in the century of *Castrati* and *Cicisbei*, of wanton Casanovas and neurotic Rousseaus and effeminate *abbés*.

It would be a mistake, however, to confine our appreciation of Tiepolo to this one note of his affinity to Veronese. Every artist of such calibre has a distinction of his own. To seize this characteristic and personal quality with absolute certainty in the case of Tiepolo requires some patience of analysis. At first we are tempted to find it in those vast decorative schemes for ceilings—apotheoses of Saints or Heroes, with flying Angels, allegorical figures upon clouds and cornices, in all possible attitudes of violent movement and perilous foreshortening: works in the *barocco* taste of the Italian decadence, upon which the noble artist spent too much of his energy and time. The contrast between these soulless compositions and the serious frescoes of the Labia palace is very striking; and here indeed we have something in quite a different key from that of Veronese's art. But if this had been Tiepolo's only or chief claim on our regard, he would count at best as one of the most consummate scene-painters in subordination to architectural effect, whom modern Europe has produced. His title to distinction is not here.

The specific strength of Tiepolo as an artist lay, I take it, in a peculiar and just perception of certain atmospheric and colour qualities in his Venetian birthplace; the employment of which for the realisation of very original and bold conceptions placed him in advance not only of Veronese, but also of all his contemporaries. He is the true Italian pioneer of the most modern aims and sentiments in painting. Tiepolo, in spite of his *barocco* decorative schemes, his frigid allegories and conventional "machines," was a *plein air* master in a sense of this term, which is wholly inapplicable to men like Guardi, Canaletto, Longhi. I do not mean to assert that he actually worked in the open air, or that he struggled consciously with those problems of values and relations, which tax the energies of recent naturalistic painters. His originality consisted in the fact, that he seems to have been aware of the imminence of a radical change in art-principles, and in the effort to bring *plein air* into the studio, where hitherto a conventional scheme of light and colour held undisputed sway. His key of colour, wonderfully clear and luminous, is settled by the harmonies between weather-mellowed marble, light blue sky, russet or ochre-tinted sails, vivid vegetable greens, sunburnt faces, and patches of bright hues in the costume of sailors and the common people, all subdued and softened by the pearly haze "of moisture bred," which bathes Venetian landscape in the warmth of early summer. Gazing down the Zattere, along the façade of S. Maria del Rosario, with the cypress-spires and creepers of the Dolgorouki garden for foreground, and a group of fishing boats in middle distance; these objects forming as it were an episode in the great poem of the wide-spreading canal of the Giudecca, arched over by illimitable light-irradiated heavens—taking then this point of vision on a June morning about ten, when the sun is already high above the horizon, we enter into the region of Tiepolo's artistic sympathies. He caught this aspect of his sea-girt home: and being a sincere and scientific draughtsman, he was able to place the figures of his pictures with perfect relief of modelling, in right aërial perspective, and with exact relative tone-values, in the midst of a liquid, luminous, translucent atmosphere. When he is painting at his best, not to order, but *con amore*, we do not feel, as we always feel with Titian and Veronese, that the pictorial scheme has been settled for studio-lighting, with careful adjustments of facts observed during the artist's study of external nature. On the contrary, we feel that he has detached and fixed for us a fragment of the whole wide scene around him and ourselves. In other words, Tiepolo breaks the tradition, derived from mediæval miniature through fresco, of a conventional chiaroscuro and a conventional system of decorative tinting. The living *rapport* which exists in nature between colour, light and atmosphere, is felt and reproduced by him.

I might illustrate these remarks by the famous oil-painting of Christ's Ascent to Calvary, now on view in the cast-room of the Accademia. But I prefer to take for my example a smaller canvas exhibited upon an easel beside this large one, which seems to epitomise the qualities of style on which I am insisting.*

It is a tall and narrow canvas, divided, after old Venetian custom, into two almost equal sections; the upper portion being occupied with sky and architecture, the lower with a group of figures in which the subject-interest of the composition concentrates. On the marble pavement of the palace, in the open air, kneels a female

* The picture has been lately replaced in the Church of the Apostoli, where it is very badly lighted.

saint supported by praying women, and backed by mundane figures—a hard-featured old man, a dainty page, and so forth. The saint, whose head and flowing fair hair is surrounded with an opalescent aureole, like greenish water of the lagoon flashed through with silvery sunbeams, kneels in an attitude of physical prostration. She is clearly dying, parting her lips languidly to receive the sacred wafer from the hand of a ministering priest in cope and full canonicals. He bends down to her, just as the priest bends in Domenichino's Communion of S. Jerome. An acolyte, kneeling and raising a lighted candle, supports this sacerdotal dignitary in his heavy robes of celebration. And thus two principal masses are formed for the group: the one determined by the dying saint, the other by the ministrant priest. They are connected, and carried into combination with the architecture and the sky by a gorgeously attired ecclesiastic with white hair, who stands erect between the two figure-masses and controls the colour scheme of the composition. In this man's robes a richly-glowing but subdued ochre, like gold dulled and smouldering, predominates. The saint, at his side, below him, is clothed in white, all the shades and semitones of which have been worked with greens and yellows and faint suggestions of greyish blues. It may be said at once that,

ON AN ALTAR-PIECE BY TIEPOLO

although at a distance the chromatic scheme seems singularly decisive and vigorous, yet on inspection it is impossible to discover any pure or simple hue in any portion of the picture. That *plein air* effect at which I think Tiepolo was aiming, is gained by the most subtle and adroit interworking of tint with tint; not any one of the dominant hues (except in the very highest lights) being allowed to assert its own unmodified quality. The hair of the bending priest, for instance, looks black at a certain distance. Yet it is almost entirely painted in strokes of bright blue upon a dark ground.

Examining the group of figures, in order to understand the subject of this altar-piece, we find that the saint is a woman of exquisite and natural beauty, a lily of whiteness, a princess of dignity and grace. The ashen pallor of her face shows that she has suffered some sudden and terrible shock to her vital system; and on her exquisite pure throat there is just one little stain of crimson, indicating blood. The heavy bluish lids droop downward to her ivory cheeks; and as we gaze intently, we seem to feel that they cover no eyes, but only empty orbits. This impression is so vaguely, so tenderly communicated, that at first I rebuked my fancy for having trespassed on some region of unimaginable horror, which existed not in the manly painter's mind, but in my own too curious imagination. Then I perceived upon a step below the marble platform where the saint is kneeling, a silver plate with two eyes placed upon it, and by the side thereof a bloody stiletto. It seemed, then, that the pity and terror I had taken from those drooping eyelids were not fanciful; and I christened the picture (whether rightly or wrongly I do not know, for it is not catalogued) by the title of " The Last Communion of S. Lucy."

In addition to his other qualities, Tiepolo painted like a great gentleman. There is an unmistakable note of good breeding in all his work. I do not remember to have ever found him vulgar, brutal, or *bourgeois*. And here, where he skirted the very border of the abyss of physical torment, he avoids the clumsy symbolism of mediæval painters—jocund women carrying their eyes or bleeding breasts on plates: he avoids the butcherly abominations of Italian or Flemish or French naturalists—Carravaggio's flayings, Rubens's flakes of spear-divided flesh with blood and water gushing from a gaping wound, Poussin's bowels wound like ropes on capstans by brawny varlets. Tiepolo shows proper respect for the reality of his subject, together with noble breeding and a fine sense for the limits of art, by creating a thing of beauty, which, when examined *à la loupe*, betrays a

ON AN ALTAR-PIECE BY TIEPOLO

tragic content, but does not force this in any painful way upon attention. Lovers of what is beautiful in art need not dwell upon the cruel details of the subject-matter. The picture itself suffices to give pleasure by its harmonies of wisely ordered lines and colours melting in a blaze of softened lustre.

The subject in a work of art like this counts for little; and we ought to be grateful to Tiepolo for combining so much dramatic force with such dignity in his treatment of a distressing motive. The leading motive is sufficiently suggested, but feelingly subordinated to those higher purposes of elevated pleasure for which the fine arts were created. Studying this picture, I arrive at the conclusion that Tiepolo solved a very difficult art-problem more successfully than almost any of his predecessors, and than most of their successors. Mediæval painters, such for example as Perugino, treated S. Lucy on the lines of the missal and the miniature, detaching a central symbolic motive and enlarging it. They served art by making this expansion of the technically developed themes agreeable to our sense of line and tint, without attempting to deal with the real aspects of the world, and without engaging in the strife with dramatic realism. Later masters emancipated the motive from its mediæval barrenness and infantile suggestion; they sought to evoke sensation by crude and violent exhibitions of nerve-torturing martyrdom, as when Sebastian del Piombo, in a picture at the Pitti, exposed S. Apollonia with bared breasts and two executioners preparing to snip her nipples off with iron pincers. Few, at this epoch, succeeded in creating a vision of adorable beauty with all the anguish of pain expressed in it; as Sodoma once did when he painted the pallid S. Sebastian of the Uffizi. But then comes Tiepolo, with more of realistic action, with far finer suggestions, with a firmer touch upon the supreme point in the saint's crucifixion; and yet without the slightest mediæval frigidity, without a hint of brutal and disgusting realism. When it is treated in this way, we can quit the subject, and ascend into regions of pure art, where the bare subject serves as a theme. The final meaning of Tiepolo's work lies in its interpretation of a world delightful to our senses by lines and hues, naturally derived from the great source of universal beauty: form, and stuff, and substance, flooded by the light of day; things closest to our senses, yet capable of subtlest transformation at the poet-artist's bidding.

This little picture, then, which I have chosen for my text, is a miracle of all perfections in the painter's craft. Within a narrow space the master has played with architectural perspective, with atmosphere, with consummate drawing of the human form, with cunning composition ; and these essentials of art he has used as preludes to the revel of his light and colour sense. When the details have been keenly scrutinised and studied, we return to the first impression made upon us by the first sight of the canvas. Its marvellous luminosity : its multiplication of low-toned colours in a scheme of yellow and green, delicately heightened by audacious flakes of red (as on the jewel of S. Lucy's bosom), and turquoise blue, and crimson (in the page's jacket), and blots of *acqua-marina*—gemmily imposed upon the thick impasto of the dominant ochres, and flooded with light in which the melody of tone throbs and quivers.

A critic of art, a describer, finds no words to communicate the passion of a picture so exalted by its maker's vivid grasp upon the beauty of the world he felt so keenly in one aspect of its many-sided fascination.

It is impossible that another Tiepolo should be born again : one who preserved the great Italian tradition, the solemn *cantilena* of the Venetian religious style ; transforming this at the touch of his magician's wand into something which the newest schools can recognise as breathed upon by the spirit they obey.

THE DANTESQUE AND PLATONIC IDEALS OF LOVE

I

THE sexcentenary of Beatrice Portinari, which was celebrated two years ago at Florence, compelled the student of Dante's life and writings once more to consider the relation of the poet to his lady. Are we to accept as truths of history the facts related by Boccaccio—namely, that Dante's father took him at the age of nine to a May-day feast in the house of Folco Portinari, and that there he beheld Beatrice, the daughter of his host, for the first time? "She was a child of eight then," says Boccaccio, "more fit to be an angel than a girl." Are we to accept the incidents of the "Vita Nuova" literally? In that record of his earliest life experience, Dante says that love on this occasion took possession of his soul, and that henceforth he worshipped Beatrice, till the day of her death, with steadfast silent adoration. To see her pass upon the streets, to receive her salutation, to sympathise with her at a distance in her joys and griefs, sufficed to keep the flame of spiritual passion alive in his heart, until that day in the year 1290, six centuries ago, when "the Lord of Justice called my most gracious lady to be glorious beneath the banner of that blessed Queen Mary whose name was always of greatest reverence in the words of saintly Beatrice." It does not appear from anything he tells us of his youthful years that they conversed together; and of love in the common acceptation of that term it is clear there was no question. Are we then to believe that the inspiring lady of the Convito, who typifies philosophy, that the Beatrice of the Paradise, who is certainly Divine Wisdom, was still this same daughter of Folco Portinari? During those years of severe studies, of political activity, of exile, after his marriage and the birth of several children, did Dante still cherish the memory of Beatrice, whom he had worshipped at a distance from his tenth to his twenty-fifth year? How are we to explain the fact, that a love, so immaterial, so visionary, begotten in the tender days of childhood, and fed with aliment so unsubstantial, exercised this enduring influence over a man of Dante's stamp—severe, precise, logical, austerely loyal to truth as he conceived it?

IDEALS OF LOVE

In short, was Beatrice a woman? Or was she, as a certain school of commentators (starting with Gian Maria Filelfo, and represented in this century by the elder Rossetti, by Barlow, by Tomlinson, and others) would have us imagine— was she an ideal, an allegory?

For my own part I cannot reject the authority of Dante's contemporaries, Boccaccio and Villani, who believed in the literal meaning of the "Vita Nuova." I cannot doubt the accent of veracity in that book of youthful love. I cannot put out of sight the sonnet to Guido Cavalcanti, in which the poet, assuming for once a tone of familiarity and daily life, speaks of his lady as one whose presence in the flesh might give complete and innocent joy to her lover. The mistrust in the reality of Beatrice seems to me to have arisen partly from the false note struck by Boccaccio, and partly from Dante's own mystical habit of mind. Boccaccio could not comprehend the peculiar nature of chivalrous passion as it existed in natures more metaphysical than his own. And Dante from the very beginning, in his language about love, in his idealisation of the woman whom he loved, introduced an element of allegory. Even in the "Vita Nuova" she is not merely a beautiful and gracious girl, but a spiritual being, round whom his highest and deepest thoughts spontaneously crystallise. She is the living ensign of a power more potent than herself, of something vital in the universe for Dante; of Love, in fact, which for her lover included all his noblest impulses and purest strivings after the ideal life. Early in his boyhood he formed this habit of regarding Beatrice; and after her death, in spite of all temporal changes, the habit was continued; so that at last she became in fact what critics of the allegorical interpretation wish to believe she always had been—a symbol. Still, even to the last, even in the pageant of the Purgatory and the ascent through Paradise, Beatrice retains a portion of her original womanhood. She is never wholly transmuted into allegory.

It is only by adhering steadily to these conceptions—to the thought of Beatrice as a real woman, whom Dante really selected to love after the singular fashion of his age; and to the thought of her submitted to an allegorising process from the earliest in her lover's mind—that we can arrive at sound critical conclusions on this problem. Our main difficulty is to throw ourselves back by sympathy and intelligence into the mood of emotion which made the poet's attitude possible. In other words, we have to try to comprehend that very peculiar form of philosophical enthusiasm which the chivalrous love of mediæval Christendom assumed in Italy.

In the case of Dante, this presents itself to our imagination under conditions of almost insuperable unintelligibility, owing to the specific qualities of his unique genius. The other poets of his period, Cino, Guido Guinicelli, Guido Cavalcanti, afterwards Petrarch, approached love from the same points of view—of mysticism, allegory, metaphysical interpretation—each, according to his character and temperament, blending the memory of the woman who had stirred passion in his soul with those aspiring thoughts and exalted emotions which were then considered to be the natural offspring of respectful love, until the woman disappeared in an incense-cloud of adoration, vanished in a labyrinth of philosophical abstractions. This, so to speak, was the method of that school of poetry which, transmitted from Provence through Sicily, took upon itself a new character of intellectual subtlety at Florence and Bologna. But Dante, while he followed the method, displayed the inevitable qualities of his marked personality. We have to deal with no mere lyrist and schoolman, such as Guido Cavalcanti was. Dante is over and above all the singer of the Divine Comedy, the poet of stirring dramatic passages, of concrete images, of firm grasp on all external and internal facts. The realistic veracity of his genius applied to the delineation of an actual emotion so spiritual as that of his for Beatrice, has misled people into thinking that he cannot be telling the truth. There are strains of feeling so ethereal and impalpable (as there are qualities of pitch in sound so fine) that the ordinary sense does not perceive them. Dante, in the "Vita Nuova" and the "Rime," expresses such a feeling; and he further complicates our difficulty by doing so to a great extent indirectly, employing the method of his school, allegorising, transmuting love-thoughts into metaphysical conceptions, confounding the simple propositions of a natural emotion with the corollaries from those propositions in the lover's mind. Beatrice is not only Beatrice, Portinari's daughter and Simone's wife. She is also all that the poet-philosopher learned and saw and loved of beautiful or good or true; the whole of which, as springing from her influence, he carries to her credit, and worships under her sign and symbol.

This, I repeat, is a difficult attitude of mind for us modern men, with our positive conceptions, to assimilate. In order to approach the task more easily, it may be well to consider another type of amorous enthusiasm which once flourished in the world for a short season, and which also assumed the philosophical mantle. I allude to that specific type of Greek love which Plato expounds in the "Phædrus" and "Symposium."

IDEALS OF LOVE

Greek love and chivalrous love form two extraordinary and exceptional phases of psychological experience. By comparing them in their points of similarity and points of difference, we may come to understand more of that peculiar enthusiasm which they possessed in common, which made love in either case a ladder for scaling the higher fortresses of intellectual truth, and which it is now well-nigh impossible for us to realise as actual.

II

In order to understand the Platonic and the Florentine enthusiasm, the love of the "Symposium" and the love of the "Vita Nuova," we must begin by studying the conditions under which they were severally elaborated.

Platonic love, in the true sense of that phrase, was the affection of a man for a man; and it grew out of antecedent customs which had obtained from very distant times in Hellas. Homer excludes this emotion from his picture of society in the heroic age. The tale of Patroclus and Achilles in the "Iliad" does not suggest the interpretation put on it by later generations; and the legend of Ganymede is related without a hint of personal desire. It has therefore been assumed that what is called Greek love was unknown at the time when the Homeric poems were composed. This argument, however, is not conclusive; for Homer, in his theology, suppressed the darker and cruder elements of Greek religion, which certainly survived from ancient savagery, and which prevailed long after the supposed age of those poems. An eclectic spirit of refinement presided over the redaction of the "Iliad" and the "Odyssey"; and the other omission I have mentioned may possibly be due to the same cause. The orator Æschines, in his critique of the Achilleian story, adopts this explanation. Unhappily for the science of comparative literature, we have lost the Cyclic poems. But there is reason to believe that these contained direct allusions to the passion in question. Otherwise, Æschylus, the conservative, and Sophocles, the temperate, would hardly have written tragedies (the "Myrmidons" and the "Lovers of Achilles") which brought Greek love upon the Attic stage. If the "Iliad" had been his sole authority, Æschylus could not have made Achilles burst forth into that cry of "unhusbanded grief" over the corpse of his dead comrade, which Lucian and Athenæus have preserved for us.

However this may be, masculine love, as the Greeks called it, appeared at an early age in

Hellas. We find it localised in several places, and consecrated by divers legends of the gods. Yet none of the later Greeks could give a distinct account of its origin or importation. There are critical grounds for supposing that the Dorians developed this custom in their native mountains (the home of Achilles and the region where it still survives), and that they carried it upon their migration to Peloponnesus. At any rate, in Crete and Sparta, it speedily became a social institution, regulated by definite laws and sanctioned by the State. In each country a youth who had no suitor lost in public estimation. The elder, in these unions of friends, received the name of " inspirer" or " lover," the younger that of " hearer " or " admired." When the youth grew up and went to battle with his comrade, he assumed the title of bystander in the ranks. I have not space to dwell upon the minute laws and customs by which Dorian love was governed. Suffice it to say that in all of them we discern the intention of promoting a martial spirit in the population, securing a manly education for the young, and binding the male members of the nation together by bonds of mutual affection. In earlier times at least care was taken to secure the virtues of loyalty, self-respect, and permanence in these relations. In short, masculine love constituted the chivalry of primitive Hellas, the stimulating and exalting enthusiasm of her sons. It did not exclude marriage, nor had it the effect of lowering the position of women in society, since it is notorious that in those Dorian States where the love of comrades became an institution, women received more public honour and enjoyed fuller liberty and power over property than elsewhere.

The military and chivalrous nature of Greek love is proved by the myths and more or less historical legends which idealised its virtues. Herakles, the Dorian demigod, typified by his affection for young men and by his unselfish devotion to humanity what the Spartan and Cretan warriors demanded from this emotion. The friendships of Theseus and Peirithous, of Orestes and Pylades, of Damon and Pythias, comrades in arms and faithful to each other to the death, embalmed the memory of lives ennobled by masculine affection. Nearly every city had some tale to tell of emancipation from tyranny, of prudent legislation, or of heroic achievements in war, inspired by the erotic enthusiasm. When Athens laboured under a grievous curse and pestilence, two lovers, Cratinus and Aristodemus, devoted their lives to the salvation of the city. Two lovers, Harmodius and Aristogeiton, shook off the bondage of the Peisistratidæ. Philolaus and Diocles gave laws to Thebes. Another Diocles won everlasting glory in a fight at Megara. Chariton and Melanippus resisted the tyranny of Phalaris at Agrigentum. Cleomachus, inspired by passion, restored freedom to the town of Chalkis. All these men were lovers of the Greek type. Tyrants, says an interlocutor in one of Plato's dialogues, tremble before lovers. Glorying in their emotion, the Greeks pronounced it to be the crowning virtue of free men, the source of gentle and heroic actions, the heirloom of Hellenic civilisation, in which barbarians and slaves had and could have no part or lot. The chivalry of which I am speaking powerfully influenced Greek history. All the Spartan kings and generals grew up under the institution of Dorian comradeship. Epameinondas and Alexander were notable lovers; and the names of their comrades are recorded. When Greek liberty expired upon the Plain of Chæronea, the Sacred Band of Thebans, all of whom were lovers, fell dead to a man; and Philip wept as he beheld their corpses, crying aloud : "Perish the man who thinks that these men either did or suffered what is shameful." It powerfully influenced Greek art. Pindar and Sophocles were lovers; Pindar died in the arms of Theoxenos, whose praise he sang in the Skolion of which we have a characteristic fragment. Pheidias carved the name of his beloved

Pantarkes on the chryselephantine statue of Olympian Zeus. Æschylus, as we have seen, wrote one of his most popular tragedies upon the affection of Achilles for Patroclus. Solon, Demosthenes, Æschines, among statesmen and orators, made no secret of a feeling which they regarded as the highest joy in life and the source of exalted enthusiasm.

Greek love, as I have shown, was in its origin and essence masculine, military, chivalrous. However repugnant to modern taste may be the bare fact that this passion existed and flourished in the highest-gifted of all races, yet it was clearly neither an effeminate depravity nor a sensual vice. Still such an emotion, being abnormal, could not prevail and dominate the customs of a whole nation without grave drawbacks. Very close to the chivalry of Hellas lurked a formidable social evil, just as adultery was intertwined with the chivalry of mediæval Europe. Adultery was not occasionally, but so to speak continually, mixed up with the feudal love *de par amour*. One ingenious writer, Vernon Lee, even maintains that adultery was the very ground on which that love flourished. In like manner, another immorality was, not occasionally, but continually mixed up with Greek love, was the soil on which it flourished. Therefore in those States especially, like Athens, where the love in question had not been moralised by prescribed laws, did it tend to degenerate. And it was just here, at Athens, that it received the metaphysical idealisation which justifies us in comparing it to the Italian form of mediæval chivalry. Socrates, says Maximus Tyrius, pitying the state of young men, and wishing to raise their affections from the mire into which they were declining, opened a way for the salvation of their souls through the very love they then abused. Whether Socrates was really actuated by these motives, cannot be affirmed with certainty. At any rate, he handled masculine love with robust originality, and prepared the path for Plato's philosophical conception of passion as an inspiration leading men to the divine idea.

I have observed that in Dorian chivalry the lover was called "inspirer," and the beloved "hearer." It was the man's duty to instruct the lad in manners, feats of arms, trials of strength and music. This relation of the elder to the younger is still assumed to exist by Plato. But he modifies it in a way peculiar to himself, upon the consideration of which I must now enter, since we have reached the very point of contact between Plato's and Dante's enthusiasm.

Socrates, as interpreted in the Platonic dialogues entitled "Phædrus" and "Symposium," sought to direct and elevate a moral force, an enthusiasm, an exaltation of the emotions, which already existed as the highest form of feeling in the Greek race. In the earlier of those dialogues he describes the love of man for youth as a madness, or divine frenzy, not different in quality from that which inspires prophets and poets. The soul he compares to a charioteer guiding a pair of winged horses, the one of noble, the other of ignoble breed. Under this metaphor is veiled the psychological distinctions of reason, generous impulse, and carnal appetite. Composed of these triple elements, the soul has shared in former lives the company of gods, and has gazed on beauty, wisdom, and goodness, the three most eminent manifestations of the divine, in their pure essence. But, sooner or later, during the course of her celestial wanderings, the soul is dragged to earth by the baseness of the carnal steed. She enters a form of flesh, and loses the pinions which enabled her to soar. Yet even in her mundane life (that obscure and confused state of existence which Plato elsewhere compares to a dark cave visited only by shadows of reality) she may be reminded of the heavenly place from which she fell, and of the glorious visions of divinity she there enjoyed. No mortal senses, indeed, could bear the sight of truth or goodness or beauty in their undimmed splendour. Yet earthly things in which truth, goodness, and beauty are incarnate, touch the soul to adoration, stimulate the growth of her wings, and set her on the upward path whereby she will revert to God. The lover has this opportunity when he beholds the person who awakes his passion; for the human body is of all earthly things that in which real beauty shines most clearly. When Plato proceeds to say that "philosophy in combination with affection for young men" is the surest method for attaining to the higher spiritual life, he takes for granted that reason, recognising the divine essence of beauty, encouraging the generous impulses of the heart, curbing the carnal appetite, converts the mania of love into an instrument of edification. Passionate friends, bound together in the chains of close yet temperate comradeship, seeking always to advance in wisdom, self-restraint, and intellectual illumination, prepare themselves for the celestial journey. "When the end comes, they are light and ready to fly away, having conquered in one of the three heavenly or truly Olympian victories. Nor can human discipline or divine inspiration confer any greater blessing on man than this." Moreover, even should they decline toward sensuality and taste those pleasures on which the vulgar set great store, they, too, will pass from life, "unwinged indeed, but eager to soar, and thus obtain no mean reward of love and madness."

The doctrine of the "Symposium" is not different, except that here Socrates, professing to report the teaching of a wise woman Diotima, assumes a loftier tone, and attempts a sublimer flight. Love, he says, is the child of Poverty and Contrivance, deriving something from both his father and his mother. He lacks all things, and has the wit to gain all things. Love too, when touched by beauty, desires to procreate; and if the mortal lover be one whose body alone is creative, he betakes himself to woman and begets children; but if the soul be the chief creative principle in the lover's nature, then he turns to young men of "fair and noble and well-nurtured spirit," and in them begets the immortal progeny of high thoughts and generous emotions. The same divine frenzy of love, which forms the subject of the "Phædrus," is here again treated as the motive force which starts the soul upon her journey towards the region of essential truth. Attracted by what is beautiful, the lover first dedicates himself to one youth in whom beauty is apparent; next he is led to perceive that beauty in all fair forms is a single quality; he then passes to the conviction that intellectual is superior to physical beauty; and so by degrees he attains the vision of a single science, which

IDEALS OF LOVE

is the science of beauty everywhere, or the worship of the divine under one of its three main attributes.

The lesson which both of these Socratic dialogues seem intended to inculcate, may be summed up thus. Love, like poetry and prophecy, is a divine gift, which diverts men from the common current of their earthly lives; and in the right use of this gift lies the secret of all human excellence. The passion which grovels in the filth of sensual grossness may be transformed into a glorious enthusiasm, a winged splendour, capable of rising to the contemplation of eternal verities and reuniting the soul of man to God. How strange will it be, when once those heights of intellectual intuition have been scaled, to look down again on earth and view the human being in whom the spirit first recognised the essence of beauty.

There is a deeply rooted mysticism, an impenetrable Soofyism, in the Socratic doctrine of Erôs. And it must be borne in mind that the love of women is rigidly and expressly excluded from the scheme. The soul which has attained to the highest possible form of perfection in this life, is defined by Plato ("'Phædr." 249, A.), to be " the soul of one who has followed philosophy with flawless self-devotion, or who has combined his passion for young men with the pursuit of truth." These are the essential conditions of Platonic love; and they are so strange that Lucian, Epicurus, Cicero, and Gibbon may be pardoned for sneering at "the thin device of virtue and friendship which amused the philosophers of Athens," just as in modern times the purity of chivalrous love has been almost universally suspected.

III

It is not needful to describe the conditions of mediæval chivalry with great particularity of detail. They are better known than the conditions of Greek chivalry; and the enthusiastic love which sprang from them, though little understood, is regarded by common consent as legitimate and beneficial to society.

Chivalry must not be confounded with the feudalism out of which it emerged. It was an ideal, binding men together by common spiritual enthusiasms. We find the ground material of the chivalrous virtues in the Teutonic character. As described by Tacitus, the German races were distinguished for chastity, obedience to self-imposed laws, truth, loyalty, regard for honour more than gain, and a reverence for women amounting to idolatry. These qualities furnished a proper soil for the chivalrous emotions; and

IDEALS OF LOVE

the chivalrous investiture, whereby the young knight was consecrated to a noble life, can also be derived from Teutonic customs. "They decorate their youthful warriors with the shield and spear," says Tacitus, insisting on the sacred obligation which this ceremony imposed. Chivalry would, however, scarcely have assumed the form it did in the twelfth century but for the slowly refining influences of Christianity. In the epics of the Niblung Cycle, and in the song of Roland, there are but faint traces of its subtler spirit. The unselfishness of the true knight, his humility and obedience, his devotion to the service of the weak and helpless, his inspiration by ideals, his readiness to forgive and to show mercy—in fact, what we may call his charity in armour—sprang from Christianity. It is only in the later romances of King Arthur that these essential elements of the chivalrous spirit make themselves manifest.

"As for death," says a knight of the Round Table, "be he welcome when he cometh; but my oath and my honour, the adventure that hath fallen to me, and the love of my lady, I will lose them not."

This sentence, in a few words, expresses the attitude of a chivalrous gentleman. When King Arthur established his knights in a solemn chapter at the Court of Camelot, he "charged them never to do outrage nor murder, and alway to flee treason; also by no means to be cruel, but to give mercy unto him that asked mercy, upon pain of forfeiture of their worship and lordship of King Arthur for evermore; and always to do ladies, damosels, and gentlewomen succour upon pain of death. Also that no man take no battles in a wrong quarrel for no law, nor for worldly goods." The knights, both old and young, swore to these articles; and every year they took the oath again at the high feast of Pentecost.

As the Christian religion in general exercised a decisive influence in the formation of chivalry, so we may perhaps connect the peculiar mode of amorous enthusiasm which characterised this ideal with the worship of the maiden mother of Christ. Woman had been exalted to the throne of heaven; and it was not unnatural that woman should become an object of almost religious adoration upon earth. The names of God and of his lady were united on the lips of a true knight; for the motto of chivalry in its best period was "Dieu et ma Dame." Love came to be regarded as the source of all nobility, virtue, heroism, and self-sacrifice. " A knight may never be of prowess," says Sir Tristram, " but if he be a lover." This language precisely corresponds with the language of the Greeks regarding that other love of theirs, which nerved them for deeds of prowess, for the overthrow of tyrants, and the liberation of their fatherland.

Chivalrous love was wholly extra-nuptial and anti-matrimonial. The lady whom the knight adored and served, who received his service and rewarded his devotion, could never be his wife. She might be a maiden or a married woman ; in practice she was almost invariably the latter. But the love which united the two in bonds more firm than any other, was incompatible with marriage. The feudal courts of love in fact proclaimed that "between two married persons, Love cannot exert his powers." This is a peculiarity well worthy of notice. Not only does it at once and for ever set an end to those foolish questions which have sometimes been asked about the reasons why Dante did not marry Beatrice ; it also constitutes one of the strongest points of similarity between the chivalrous love of the ancient Greeks and that of the mediæval races. Plato, in the "Symposium," it will be remembered, asserts that the exalted love on which he is discoursing has nothing whatever to do with the "vulgar and trivial" way of matrimony. It must be excited by a person with whom connubial relations are absolutely impossible. It is a state of the soul, not an appetite ; and though the weakness of mortality may lead lovers into sensuality, such shortcomings form a distinct deviation from the ideal. Least of all can it have anything to do with those connections profitable to the State and useful to society, which involve the procreation and rearing of children, domestic cares, and the commonplace of daily duties. In theory, at any rate, both Greek and mediæval types of chivalrous emotion were pure and spiritual enthusiasms, purging the lover's soul of all base thoughts, lifting him above the bondage of the flesh, and filling him with a continual rapture.

Plato called love a "mania," an inspired frenzy. Among the chivalrous lovers of Provence, this high rapture received the name of "Joy." It will here be remembered by students of the "Morte Darthur" that the castle to which both Lancelot and Tristram carried off their ladies was Joyous Gard. The fruits of joy were bravery, courtesy, high spirit, sustained powers of endurance, delight in perilous adventure. The soul of the knight, penetrated with the fine elixir of enthusiatic love, is ready to confront all dangers, to undertake the most difficult tasks, to bear obloquy and want, the scorn of men, misunderstanding, even coldness and disdain on the part of his lady, with serene sweetness and an exalted patience. Plato's description of the lover in the "Phædrus" exactly squares with

IDEALS OF LOVE

this romantic ideal of the knight's enthusiasm. The permanent emotion, whether termed "mania" or "joy," is precisely the same in quality; and whether the object which stirred it was a young man as in Greece, or a married woman as in mediæval Europe, signified nothing.

Chivalrous love, under both its forms, did not exclude marriage, except between the lovers themselves. Lancelot and Tristram took wives, while remaining loyal to Guinevere and Iseult, their ladies. Dante had children by Gemma, and Petrarch by a concubine. Still it was the sainted Beatrice, the unattainable Laura, who received the homage of these poets and inspired their art.

In theory, then, chivalrous love of both types, the Greek and the mediæval, existed independently of the marriage tie and free from sensual affections. It was, in each case, the source of exhilarating passion; a durable ecstasy which removed the lover to a higher region, rendering him capable of haughty thoughts and valiant deeds. Both loves were originally martial, and connected with the military customs of the peoples among whom they flourished. Both, in practice and in course of time, fell below their own ideal standards, without, however, losing the high spirit, loyalty, and sense of honour, which went far to compensate for what was defective in their psychological basis. At the same time, social evils of the gravest kind were inseparable from both forms of enthusiastic feeling, because each had striven to transcend the sphere of natural duties and of normal instincts.

At this point, when feudal chivalry was tending toward the travesty which is depicted for us in "Little Jehan de Saintré," the same thing happened at Florence to its imaginative essence as had previously happened to the imaginative essence of Greek chivalry at Athens. We have seen that Greek love was originally a Dorian and soldierly passion; it had grown up in the camp: and when it lost its primal quality in the Attic circles, Socrates attempted to utilise the force he recognised in this still romantic feeling for the stimulation of a nobler intellectual life. The moral energy was there. It throbs through previous ages of Greek legend, literature, and history. But a philosophical application of this motive, which is the peculiar discovery of the Platonic Socrates, had not been attempted. That was reserved for the Athenians, and, in particular, for the school of the Academy. Precisely in like manner, chivalry, the fine but scarcely wholesome flower of feudalism, the super-subtle hybrid between savage Teutonic virtues and hyper-sensitive Christian emotions, which grew up in the mediæval castle, had been

now transplanted to the classic soil of Italy.
Italy was neither feudal nor Teutonic; and her
Christianity, for the highest of her sons, was
deeply penetrated with political and intellectual
ideas. The generous Tuscan spirits who
adopted chivalry, partly as a motive for their
art, and partly as a visionary guide in conduct
—Guido Guinicelli, Guido Cavalcanti, Cino da
Pistoja, Lapo, Dante—enamoured of its beauty,
but unable to prolong its life upon the former
line of feudal institutions, lent it the new touch
of mystical philosophy. The simple substance
of the chivalrous enthusiasm, which had taken
gracious form in the legends of Lancelot and
Tristram, of Sir Beaumains and Sir Galahad,
was refined upon and spun into a web of
allegory. The subtleties and psychological
distinctions of the troubadours received metaphysical interpretations. A nation of scholars
and of doctors, who were also artists—Dante
calls the poets of his school *dottori*—men who
were not knights or squires or mighty of their
hands, reformed, rehandled, and recast the
tradition of the love they had received from
militant subconscious predecessors. We come
thus to the remarkable fact that the last manifestation of mediæval love at Florence represents
an almost exact parallel to the last manifestation
of Greek love at Athens. In both instances, an

enthusiasm which had its root in human passion, after passing through a martial phase of evolution and becoming a social factor of importance in the raising of the race to higher spiritual power, assumes the aspect of philosophy, and connects itself with the effort of the intellect to reach the Beatific Vision. Dante, conducted by Beatrice into the circle of the Celestial Rose, proclaims the same creed as Plato when he asserts that the love of a single person, leading the soul upon the way to truth, becomes the means whereby man may ascend to the contemplation of the divine under one of its eternal aspects.

What is really remarkable in the parallel I have attempted to establish is, that the metaphysical transformation of Greek "mania" and mediæval "joy," which was effected severally at Athens and in Tuscany, took place in each case by a natural and independent process of development. We have no reason to suppose that feudal chivalry owed anything to Platonic influences, even in this its latest manifestation. It is certain, for instance, that Dante never read the "Phædrus" and the "Symposium" in the originals; and nothing shows that he was even remotely acquainted with their true substance in scholastic compendiums. The same exalted psychological condition followed similar lines of development, and reached the same result—a result which in each case is almost unintelligible to us who study it. We find the greatest difficulty in believing that Socrates was sincere, and that Dante was sincere. We turn, like Gibbon, in our perplexity about Greek love to the hypothesis of "a thin device of friendship and virtue," masking gross immorality. We turn, like the elder Rossetti and his school, in our perplexity about Dante's idealisation of Beatrice, to the hypothesis of a political or a theological allegory. But sound criticism rejects both of these hypotheses. Frankly admitting that Greek love was tainted with a vice obnoxious to modern notions, and that mediæval love was involved with adultery, the true critic will declare that, strange and incomprehensible as this must always seem, there were two brief moments, once at Athens and once at Florence, when amorous enthusiasms of an abnormal type presented themselves to natures of the noblest stamp as indispensable conditions of the progress of the soul upon the pathway toward perfection.

IV

I have dwelt in this essay more upon the similarity between Greek and mediæval love than on their difference. The identity of the psychological phenomenon is what I had to demonstrate. Yet each was distinguished by characteristics which make it seem at first sight the exact contrary of the other. The antique Platonist, as appears from numerous passages in the Platonic writings, would have despised the Petrarchist as a vulgar woman-lover. The Petrarchist would have loathed the Platonist as a moral pariah. But, though the emotion differed in external aspect, the spiritual quintessence of it was the same. Romantic passion, distilled through the alembic of philosophy, produced both at Athens and in Italy a rare and singular exaltation, which only superficial observers will deny to have been one and the same psychical condition.

The person of a beautiful youth led Plato's Socrates to follow beauty through all its epiphanies until he arrived at the notion of the universal beauty which is God. Dante, under the influence of the love he felt for Beatrice, advanced in knowledge till he grasped the divine wisdom which he then symbolically identified with the woman who had inspired him.

In addition to the radical divergence I have here indicated—a divergence of moral sentiment and social custom, which presents a curious problem to the ethical inquirer—we have to take into account the dominant conceptions of the peoples who evolved this enthusiasm. Greek religion was plastic, objective, anthropomorphic. The Greeks thought of their deities as persons, whose portraits could be carved in statues. Mediæval religion was spiritual, separating the divinity man worshipped from corporeal form, so far as this was compatible with the dogma of the incarnation. Greek philosophy, in spite of its occasional excursions into mysticism, remained positive. Mediæval philosophy eagerly embraced allegory and "anagogical interpretations."

Who shall say whether the Platonic ideal evolved from the old Greek chivalry of masculine love was ever realised in actual existence? The healthy temper of the Attic mind made it difficult for men to persuade themselves that such a state of the soul was possible. But in Italy the corresponding ideal evolved from the feudal chivalry of woman-service found a more congenial soil to root in. The long travail of the past ten centuries, the many maladies of scholastic speculation, created a favourable intellectual atmosphere. Saying one thing when you meant another, clothing simple thoughts and natural instincts with the veil of symbolism, drawing an iridescent mirage of fancy over the surface of fact by half-voluntary self-sophistications : all this was alien to the frank Greek nature, familiar to the subtleising minds of schoolmen. Accordingly the Platonic conception of Greek love soon revealed its unsubstantiality, whereas the Dantesque conception of feudal love allied itself to the symbolising tendencies of the age in art and letters, and to the hazy web-weavings of contemporary science. In Greece the Platonic ideal was rudely disavowed by average men who knew what lurked at the bottom of it. In Europe the Dantesque ideal, though no one doubted how perilously near it lay to adultery, imposed for a certain time upon society. Dante, as I have remarked before, in this, as in all things, stood apart, sharing the tendencies of his age in a general way only. His successors, while they affected to carry on the tradition of the Florentine amourists, practically reverted to the unsophisticated emotions of common humanity. Laura, in Petrarch's poems, is a very real though not a very well-defined woman, and is loved by him in a very natural manner. The climax of Boccaccio's "Amorosa Visione," after all its mysticism and allegorising, is the union of two lovers in a voluptuous embrace.

What subsists of really vital and precious in both ideals is the emotional root from which they severally sprang: in Greece the love of comrades, binding friends together, spurring them on to heroic action, and to intellectual pursuits in common; in mediæval Europe the devotion to the female sex, through manly courtesy, which raised the crudest of male appetites to a higher value.

It would also be unjust, in treating of these two ideas, to forget that the first awakening of love in true and gentle natures is a psychological moment of the utmost importance. The spiritual life of a man has not unfrequently started from this point, and his addiction to nobler aims has been occasioned by the incidence of emotion. The stimulating and quickening influence of genuine love is a very real thing; and if this were all contained in the ideals we have been comparing, no exception could be taken to them. But in both cases the psychological fact has been strained beyond its power of tension; and a simple matter of experience has been made the basis of a misleading mystical philosophy.

So then the attitude of Dante toward Beatrice must, for all practical purposes, be judged as sterile and ineffectual as the attitude assumed by Plato toward young men, loved, according to Greek custom, in the playing field or in the groves of the Academy.

It is a delusion to imagine that the human spirit is led to discover divine truths by amorous enthusiasm for a fellow-creature, however refined that impulse may be. The quagmires into which those who follow such a will-o'-the-wisp will probably flounder are only too plainly illustrated by the cynical remarks of Shelley upon Emilia Viviani, written a few days after he had composed the Platonic ravings of "Epipsychidion." Nevertheless, there are delusions, wandering fires of the imaginative reason, which, for a brief period of time, under special conditions, and in peculiarly constituted natures, have become fruitful of real and excellent results. This was the case, I take it, with both Plato and Dante.

EDWARD CRACROFT LEFROY

I

NOT long ago, a writer in *The Artist* quoted some lines of remarkable dignity and beauty by E. C. L. I felt that here was a poet unknown to me; for the verses had that peculiar quality which belongs alone to genuine inspiration. By the kindness of the editor of *The Artist* I obtained a copy of the book from which the extracts had been made. It is a thin volume, entitled "Echoes from Theocritus, and Other Sonnets." By Edward Cracroft Lefroy. London: Elliot Stock, 1885. The first thirty sonnets are composed on themes suggested by the Syracusan idyllist. Of miscellaneous sonnets there are seventy. So, whether by accident or intention, the poet rests his fame upon a century of sonnets, by far the most important of these being the seventy which do not give their title to the book.

Together with this volume came the sad intelligence that Edward Lefroy died last summer after a tedious illness. In reply to inquiries, I learned, through the courtesy of his best and oldest friend, that he was educated at Blackheath Proprietary School and at Keble College, Oxford. In 1878 he took orders. His sonnets originally appeared in three small paper-covered pamphlets, severally entitled "Echoes from Theocritus," "Cytisus and Galingale," "Sketches and Studies." They were published at Blackheath by H. Burnside, bookseller, between the years 1883 and 1884, and attracted comparatively little notice. In 1885 the same sonnets were collected under the title and description I have given above. Few of our well-known literary critics, with the exception of Mr. Andrew Lang and Mr. William Sharp, took notice of them and discerned their merit. Later on, Mr. Lefroy gave a volume of sermons to the public, and in 1885 he printed a very characteristic collection of "Addresses to Senior School-boys." He was thirty-five years of age when he died.

Though Mr. Lefroy worked as a parish clergyman both at Truro and Lambeth with the late and the present Archbishops of Canterbury, he suffered from chronic physical weakness of a distressing nature. As early as the year 1882, he learned from the best medical authority that his heart was seriously affected, and that he could not expect length of life. The pains and wearinesses of illness he bore with what a critic, writing in the *Academy*, well described as " breezy healthfulness of thought and feeling." Combining in a singular measure Hellenic cheerfulness with Christian faith and patience, he was able to await death with a spiritual serenity sweeter than the steadfastness of Stoical endurance. In one of his diaries he wrote: " The world contains, even for an invalid like me, a multitude of beautiful and inspiring things. . . . . I have always tried to live a broad life. It has been my pleasure to sympathise with all sorts and conditions of men in their labours and their recreations. Art, nature, and youth have yielded to me 'the harvest of a quiet eye.' It would be affectation to pretend that I am weary of existence . . . . but I have faith enough in my Lord to follow Him willingly where He has gone before." His sympathy with youthful strength and beauty, his keen interest in boyish games and the athletic sports of young men, seem to have kept his nature always fresh and wholesome. These qualities were connected in a remarkable way with Hellenic instincts and an almost pagan delight in nature. But Lefroy's temperament assimilated from the Christian and the Greek ideals only what is really admirable in both : discarding the asceticism of the one and the sensuousness of the other. The twofold elements in him were kindly mixed and blended in a rare beauty and purity of manliness. Writing to a friend about his Theocritean sonnets, he says that he composed them in order to relax his mind. " To a man occupied in sermon-writing and parochial visitation it is intellectual change of air to go back in thought to a pre-Christian age: and I confess that I have never been able to emancipate myself (as most clergymen do) from the classical bonds which schoolmasters and college tutors for so many years did their best to weave around me. And then I have such an intense sympathy with the joys and griefs, hopes and fears, passions and actions of 'the young life' that I find myself in closer affinity to Greek feeling than most people would. At the same time, I should be sorry to help on that Hellenic revival which some Oxford teachers desire." At another time he writes : " I find the school of Keats more congenial to my 'natural man' than the school of Keble. And in my more truthful moments the temper of Sophocles seems more akin to mine than the temper of Thomas à Kempis, though the 'Imitatio' is seldom far from my hand. I mean to struggle on to a less perishable standpoint, and hope (D.V.) to diminish the frequency of my lapses into Hellenism."

II

Indeed, Lefroy seems, through some special privilege of temperament, to have hit by instinct upon the right solution of difficult problems, which many less well-balanced natures seek after in vain, because they are too coarsely fibred, too revolutionary, or peradventure too intemperate. Thus he felt able to write candidly to a friend upon a topic which is not often discussed among men (1883): "I have an inborn admiration for beauty of form and figure. It amounts almost to a passion. And in most football teams I can find one Antinous, sometimes two or three. And surely it is very beautiful to see the rapid movement of a perfect animal, &c. Some folk would say it was a mark of sickly or diseased sentimentalism to admire any but feminine flesh. But that only proves how base is the carnality, which is now reckoned the only legitimate form. The other is far nobler, unless it be vilely prostituted : and were I painter, sculptor or poet, I would teach the world so. Platonic passion in any relationship is better than the animalism which will go to all extremes." This passage strikes the key-note to a great deal of his best poetry, and shows in how true a sense he possessed the Greek virtue of temperate self-control. Modern men refuse to admit the possibility of purity in emotions which are stimulated by the aspects of physical beauty in the male and female sex. On the banks of the Ilissus they felt and thought differently ; and Lefroy existed to prove that the Lysis and Charmides of Plato are not masterpieces of artistic hypocrisy, concealing foulness.

His opinions regarding the right way of remaining faithful to the Greek ideal of life, without sacrificing cleanliness of conduct, obedience to the law, or holiness of spirit, are fully set forth in an address on "Muscular Christianity." This was printed at Oxford in 1877 (Slatter & Rose), when the Chair of Poetry, vacated by Sir Francis Doyle, was being somewhat warmly disputed. A Rev. St. John Tyrwhitt upon that occasion wrote against what Lefroy himself called the "Hellenic revival which some Oxford teachers desire ;" and I can discern an echo of the controversy in the Address, from which I mean to quote some passages. It is mainly directed against Mr. Pater and myself, to some extent also against Matthew Arnold. But "Pater-paganism and Symonds-sophistry" —that is to say, the views expressed by Pater in the last essay of his "Studies in the History of the Renaissance," and by Symonds in the last chapter of his "Studies of Greek Poets : Second Series"—are the principal objects of his attack. "What Mr. Symonds and Mr. Pater, and their followers, advise us to do," he says, "may be summed up in a single sentence : 'Act according to the promptings of nature, and you cannot go wrong.' .... In the present case, what is meant by the term 'nature'? Is it Anglo-Byzantine (as Mr. Tyrwhitt would say) for the worst passions and most carnal inclination of humanity? I fear that there is too much reason to dread an affirmative answer. .... I have called the new religion a pseudo-Hellenism, and for this reason: it seems to differ in a very important respect from Hellenism properly so-called. The Greeks had at least an ideal standard, that which they indicated by the term τὸ καλόν. Unquestionably they often fell short of it, not only in their practice, but in their doctrine on particular points ; but there is no inconsistency in the general teaching of their greatest philosophers, or in the avowed aim of their statesmen and legislators. They all pointed to the honourable, the comely, the beautiful, in every department of thought and action. They would not have tolerated for a moment a philosophy which bade each man follow freely the bent of his own unchastened disposition, or encouraged the cultivation of merely sensual faculties, without an equal training of man's diviner instincts."

I need not discuss the question how far Lefroy was just to either Mr. Pater or myself, as regards our doctrine and our practice; because I have not introduced this passage with any polemical object, but only with the view of making his position clear, and of showing how decidedly he disagreed with the prominent "Hellenisers" of his period. It was both the strength and the weakness of Lefroy's philosophy that he began by postulating the Christian faith as a divinely appointed way of surmounting the corruption and imperfection of nature. His strength; because he undoubtedly lived by this faith. His weakness; because it is impossible to demonstrate or to maintain that Christianity has this efficacy. "Muscular Christianity," to use his own phrase, "includes all that is brightest in Hellenism, and all that is purest in Hebraism." Alas! It was not Muscular Christianity, but one Muscular Christian, Lefroy himself, who included these two excellences.

III

There is a strong personal accent in all Lefroy's writing; the "breezy healthfulness of thought and feeling" which his reviewer noted; the untainted Hellenism broadening and clarifying

Christian virtues, which I have attempted to describe.

This attitude of mind is sufficiently well set forth in the last sonnet of the series. It is entitled "An Apology," and may here be cited, although in form and language it falls below the level of Lefroy's best writing:

> "*I hold not lightly by this world of sense,*
> *So full it is of things that make me cheer.*
> *I deem that mortal blind of soul and dense,*
> *To whom created joys are less than dear.*
> *The heaven we hope for is not brought more near*
> *By spurning drops of love that filter thence:*
> *In Nature's prism some purple beams appear,*
> *Of unrevealèd light the effluence.*
> *Then count me not, O yearning hearts, to blame*
> *Because at Beauty's call mine eyes respond,*
> *Nor soon convict me of ignoble aim,*
> *Who in the schools of life am frankly fond;*
> *For out of earth's delightful things we frame*
> *Our only visions of the world beyond.*"

Some of Lefroy's finest work is done in the key suggested by this sonnet. He felt that life itself is more than literature: the real poems are not what we sing, but what we feel and see. This thought, which is indeed the base-note of all Walt Whitman's theories upon art, is admirably rendered in "From Any Poet" (No. xxxvii.):

> "Oh, Fair and Young, we singers only lift
> A mirror to your beauty dimly true,
> And what you gave us, that we give to you,
> And in returning minimise the gift.
> We trifle like an artist brought to view
> The nuggets gleaming in a golden drift,
> Who, while the busy miners sift and sift,
> Will take his idle brush and paint a few.
> O Young and Glad, O Shapely, Fair, and Strong,
> Yours is the soul of verse to make, not mar !
> In you is loveliness : to you belong
> Glory and grace : we sing but what you **are**.
> Pleasant the song perchance ; but oh, how far
> The beauty sung of doth excel the song."

Feeling this, Lefroy felt, like Alfred de Musset, that the poet's true applause is praise bestowed upon him by the young :

> "O hearts of youth, so brightly, frankly true,
> To gods and bards alike your praise is dear ;
> Though wreaths from adult hands be all unseized,
> Our crowns are crowns indeed if thrown by you."

These lines, from a sonnet entitled "A Story of Aurelius" (No. xxxviii.), suffer by their severance from the rest of the poem. It may be said, indeed, in passing, that, spontaneous and unstudied as his work appears, Lefroy had a fine sense of unity. None of his pieces, to my mind, can be rightly estimated, except in their total effect. I will illustrate this by quoting at full "Bill : A Portrait" (No. xxxvi.) :

> "I know a lad with sun-illumined eyes,
> Whose constant heaven is fleckless of a cloud ;
> He treads the earth with heavy steps and proud,
> As if the gods had given him for a prize
> Its beauty and its strength. What money buys
> Is his ; and his the reverence unavowed
> Of toiling men for men who never bowed
> Their backs to any burden anywise.
> And if you talk of pain, of doubt, of ill,
> He smiles and shakes his head, as who should say,
> 'The thing is black, or white, or what you will:
> Let Folly rule, or Wisdom : any way
> I am the dog for whom this merry day
> Was made, and I enjoy it.' That is Bill."

The grace of this composition is almost rustic, the music like to that of some old ditty piped by shepherds in the shade. The subrisive irony, the touch of humour, the quiet sympathy with Nature's and Fortune's gilded darling, give it a peculiar raciness. But after all is said, it leaves a melody afloat upon the brain, a savour on the mental palate. Only lines four and five seem to interrupt the rhythm by sibilants and a certain poverty of phrase—as though (which was perhaps the case) two separate compositions had been patched together.

A companion portrait, this time of a maiden, may be placed beside it—"Flora" (No. xxxv.):

> "Some faces scarce are born of earth, they say ;
> Thine is not one of them, and yet 'tis fair ;

>   *Showing the buds of hope in soft array,*
>   *Which presently will burst and blossom there;*
>   *Now small as bells that Alpine meadows bear,—*
>   *Too low for any boisterous wind to sway.*
>   *Why should we think it shame for youth to wear*
>   *A beauty portioned from the natural day?*
>   *'Tis thine to teach us what dull hearts forget,*
>   *How near of kin we are to springing flowers.*
>   *The sap from Nature's stem is in us yet;*
>   *Young life is conscious of uncancelled powers.*
>   *And happy they who, ere youth's sun has set,*
>   *Enjoy the golden unreturning hours."*

In all these sonnets there are charming single lines:

> "*How near of kin we are to springing flowers.*"

Of children, in another place, he says:

> "*To you the glory and to us the debt.*"

And again, in yet another sonnet:

> "*We press and strive and toil from morn till eve;*
> *From eve to morn our waking thoughts are grim.*
> *Were children silent, we should half believe*
> *That joy were dead—its lamp would burn so dim.*"

This special sympathy with what he called "the young life" finds noble expression in four sonnets dedicated to the sports of boyhood. Here is "A Football Player" (No. xxvii.):

"If I could paint you, friend, as you stand there,
Guard of the goal, defensive, open-eyed,
Watching the tortured bladder slide and glide
Under the twinkling feet; arms bare, head bare,
The breeze a-tremble through crow-tufts of hair;
Red-brown in face, and ruddier having spied
A wily foeman breaking from the side;
Aware of him—of all else unaware :
If I could limn you as you leap and fling
Your weight against his passage, like a wall;
Clutch him, and collar him, and rudely cling
For one brief moment till he falls—you fall :
My sketch would have what Art can never give—
Sinew and breath and body; it would live."

The "Cricket-Bowler" follows (No. xxviii.):

" Two minutes' rest till the next man goes in!
The tired arms lie with every sinew slack
On the mown grass. Unbent the supple back,
And elbows apt to make the leather spin
Up the slow bat and round the unwary shin—
In knavish hands a most unkindly knack;
But no guile shelters under this boy's black
Crisp hair, frank eyes, and honest English skin.
Two minutes only. Conscious of a name,
The new man plants his weapon with profound
Long-practised skill that no mere trick may scare.
Not loth, the rested lad resumes the game :
The flung ball takes one madding tortuous bound,
And the mid-stump three somersaults in air."

The third, not so perfect in execution, celebrates the runner's noble strife. It is called "Before the Race" (No. xxix.) :

"*The impatient starter waxeth saturnine.*
'*Is the bell cracked?*' *he cries. They make it sound:
And six tall lads break through the standers round.
I watch with Mary while they form in line;
White jerseyed all, but each with some small sign,
A broidered badge or shield with painted ground,
And one with crimson kerchief sash-wise bound;
I think we know that token, neighbour mine.
Willie, they call you best of nimble wights;
Yet brutal Fate shall whelm in slippery ways
Two soles at least. Will it be you she spites?
Ah well! 'Tis not so much to win the bays.
Uncrowned or crowned, the struggle still delights;
It is the effort, not the palm we praise.*"

Very finely conceived and splendidly expressed is the fourth of these athletic sonnets, which connects æsthetic impressions with underlying moral ideas. "A Palæstral Study" (No. xxxi.):

"*The curves of beauty are not softly wrought:
These quivering limbs by strong hid muscles held
In attitudes of wonder, and compelled
Through shapes more sinuous than a sculptor's thought,
Tell of dull matter splendidly distraught,
Whisper of mutinies divinely quelled,—
Weak indolence of flesh, that long rebelled,
The spirit's domination bravely taught.
And all man's loveliest works are cut with pain.
Beneath the perfect art we know the strain,
Intense, defined, how deep soe'er it lies.
From each high masterpiece our souls refrain,*

*Not tired of gazing, but with stretchèd eyes
Made hot by radiant flames of sacrifice."*

I think it will be felt, from these examples, that in Lefroy's now almost forgotten work a true poet drew authentic inspiration from the beautiful things which lie nearest to the artist's vision in the life of frank and simple human beings. His sonnets rank high in that region of Art which I have elsewhere called "democratic." The sensibility to subjects of this sort may be frequent among us ; but the power of seizing on their essence, the faculty for lifting them into the æsthetic region without marring their wilding charm, are not common. For this reason, because just here seems to lie his originality, I have dwelt upon this group of poems. Their Neo-Hellenism is so pure and modern, their feeling for physical beauty and strength is so devoid of sensuality, their tone is so right and yet so warmly sympathetic, that many readers will be grateful to a singer, distinguished by rare personal originality, who touched common and even carnal things with such distinction. I might enforce this argument by quoting "The New Cricket Ground," "Childhood and Youth," "In the Cloisters : Winchester College." But, as the Greeks said, the half is more than the whole.

IV

The thirty " Echoes from Theocritus" are all penetrated with that purged Hellenic sentiment which was the note of Lefroy's genius. They are exquisite cameos in miniature carved upon fragments broken from the idylls; nor do I disagree with a critic who said, when they first appeared, that "rarely has the great pastoral poet been so freely transmuted without loss of his spell." Nevertheless, these sonnets have not the same personal interest, nor, in my opinion, the same artistic importance, as others in which the poet's fancy dealt more at large with themes suggested to him by his study of the Greek past. Take this, for instance: "Something Lost" (No. xviii.):

> "*How changed is Nature from the Time antique!*
> *The world we see to-day is dumb and cold;*
> *It has no word for us. Not thus of old*
> *It won heart-worship from the enamoured Greek.*
> *Through all fair forms he heard the Beauty speak;*
> *To him glad tidings of the Unknown were told*
> *By babbling runlets, or sublimely rolled*
> *In thunder from the cloud-enveloped peak.*
> *He caught a message at the oak's great girth,*
> *While prisoned Hamadryads weirdly sang:*
> *He stood where Delphi's Voice had chasm-birth,*

*And o'er strange vapour watched the Sibyl hang;
Or where, 'mid throbbing of the tremulous earth,
The caldrons of Dodona pulsed and rang."*

Here we feel that Lefroy (like Wordsworth when he yearned for Triton rising in authentic vision from the sea) had his soul lodged in Hellas. Of how many English poets may not this be said? " Come back, ye wandering Muses, come back home!" Landor was right. The home of the imagination of the artist is in Greece. Gray, Keats, Shelley, even Byron, Landor, Wordsworth, even Matthew Arnold, all the great and good poets who have passed away from us, signified this truth in one way or in another, each according to his quality. It was the distinction of Lefroy that he "came back home" with a peculiarly fresh and child-like perception of its charm. Seeking to define his touch upon Hellenic things, I light upon this barren and scholastic formula : he had a spiritual apperception of sensuous beauty. The strong, clear music which throbbed so piercingly, so passionately, round the Isles of Greece, reached his sense attenuated and refined—like the notes of the Alpine horn, after ascending and tingling through a thousand feet of woods and waterfalls and precipices. Here is the echo of it in his sonnet, " On the Beach in November " (No. xvii.) :

"My heart's Ideal, that somewhere out of sight
Art beautiful and gracious and alone,—
Haply where blue Saronic waves are blown
On shores that keep some touch of old delight,—
How welcome is thy memory, and how bright,
To one who watches over leagues of stone
These chilly northern waters creep and moan
From weary morning unto weary night.
O Shade-form, lovelier than the living crowd,
So kind to votaries, yet thyself unvowed,
So free to human fancies, fancy-free,
My vagrant thought goes out to thee, to thee,
As, wandering lonelier than the Poet's cloud,
I listen to the wash of this dull sea."

How he could convey a single Greek suggestion into the body of an English poem may be exemplified by "A Thought from Pindar" (No. xxxix.) :

"Twin immortalities man's art doth give
To man; both fair; both noble; one supreme.
The sculptor beating out his portrait scheme
Can make the marble statue breathe and live;
Yet with a life cold, silent, locative;
It cannot break its stone-eternal dream,
Or step to join the busy human stream,
But dwells in some high fane a hieroglyph.
Not so the poet. Hero, if thy name
Lives in his verse, it lives indeed. For then
In every ship thou sailest passenger
To every town where aught of soul doth stir,
Through street and market borne, at camp and game,
And on the lips and in the hearts of men!"

The contrast between the powers of two rival arts, sculpture and poetry, to confer immortal fame upon some noble agent in the world's drama, has been well conceived and forcibly presented.

Like all poets who have confined their practice mainly to contemplative and meditative forms of verse, Lefroy reflected on the nature of art. That he was not in theory "the idle singer of an idle day" may be gathered from a sonnet entitled " Art that Endures " (No. lxviii.) :

> "*Marble of Paros, bronze that will not rust,*
> *Onyx or agate—sculptor, choose thy block!*
> *Not clay nor wax nor perishable stock*
> *Of earthy stones can yield a virile bust*
> *Keen-edged against the centuries. Strive thou must*
> *In molten brass or adamantine rock*
> *To carve the strenuous shape which shall not mock*
> *Thy faith by crumbling dust upon thy dust.*
> *Poet, the warning comes not less to thee!*
> *Match well thy metres with a strong design.*
> *Let noble themes find nervous utterance. Flee*
> *The frail conceit, the weak mellifluous line.*
> *High thoughts, hard forms, toil, rigour,—these be thine*
> *And steadfast hopes of immortality.*"

With this lofty conception of the spirit in which the artist should approach his task, Lefroy did not exaggerate his own capacity as poet or seek to exalt his function. A sonnet called

"The Torch-Bearer" (No. lxvi.) expresses, in a charming metaphor, the thought that poetry is but the soul's light cast upon the world for other souls to see by:

> "*In splendour robed for some court-revelry*
> *A monarch moves when eve is on the wane.*
> *His faithful lieges flock their prince to see,*
> *And strive to pierce the gathering shade—in vain.*
> *But lo, a torch! And now the brilliant train*
> *Is manifest. Who may the bearer be?*
> *Not great himself, he maketh greatness plain.*
> *To him this praise at least. What more to me?*
> *Mine is a lowly Muse. She cannot sing*
> *A pageant or a passion; cannot cry*
> *With clamorous voice against an evil thing,*
> *And break its power; but seeks with single eye*
> *To follow in the steps of Love, her King,*
> *And hold a light for men to see Him by.*"

In another place (No. i.) he disclaims his right or duty to attack the higher paths of poesy, saying of his Muse:

> "*She hath no mind for 'freaks upon the fells,'*
> *No wish to hear the storm-wind rattling by:*
> *She loves her cowslips more than immortelles,*
> *Her garden-clover than the abysmal sky:*
> *In a green dell her chosen sweetheart dwells:*
> *The mountain-height she must not, does not, try.*"

That sense of inadequacy which every modest worker feels from time to time, when he compares "this man's art or that man's scope" with his own performance, and the reaction from its benumbing oppression under the influence of healthier reflection, are expressed with delightful spontaneity in " Two Thoughts" (No. xliii.) :

> "*When I reflect how small a space I fill*
> *In this great teeming world of labourers,*
> *How little I can do with strongest will,*
> *How marred that little by most hateful blurs,—*
> *The fancy overwhelms me, and deters*
> *My soul from putting forth so poor a skill:*
> *Let me be counted with those worshippers*
> *Who lie before God's altar and are still.*
> *But then I think (for healthier moments come)*
> *This power of will, this natural force of hand,—*
> *What do they mean, if working be not wise?*
> *Forbear to weigh thy work, O Soul! Arise,*
> *And join thee to that nobler, sturdier band*
> *Whose worship is not idle, fruitless, dumb.*"

V

It was not to be expected that a man who vibrated so deeply and truly to the beauty of the world and to the loveliness of "the young life," and who was himself condemned to life-long sickness with no prospect but the grave upon this planet, should not have left some utterances upon the problems of death and thwarted vitality. It must be remembered, however, that Lefroy was a believing Christian, and for him the tomb was, therefore, but a doorway opened into regions of eternal life. It is highly characteristic of the man that, in his poetry, he made no vulgar appeal to the principles of his religious creed, but remained within the region of that Christianised Stoicism I have attempted to define. We feel this strongly in the sonnets "To An Invalid" (No. liv.), "On Reading a Poet's Life" (No. lix.), and "The Dying Prince" (No. xlvii.). All of these, for their intrinsic merits, are worthy of citation. But space fails; and I would fain excite some curiosity for lovely things to be discovered by the reader when a full edition of Lefroy's "Remains" appears. I shall, therefore, content myself with the transcription of the following most original poem upon the old theme of "Quem Di Diligunt" (No. lvii.) :

"*O kiss the almond-blossom on the rod!*
A thing has gone from us that could not stay.
At least our sad eyes shall not see one day
All baseness treading where all beauty trod.
O kiss the almond-blossom on the rod!
For this our budding Hope is caught away
From growth that is not other than decay,
To bloom eternal in the halls of God.
And though of subtler grace we saw no sign,

No glimmer from the yet unrisen star,—
Full-orbed he broke upon the choir divine,
Saints among saints beyond the golden bar,
Round whose pale brows new lights of glory shine—
The aureoles that were not and that are."

The artistic value of Lefroy's work is great. That first attracted me to him, before I knew what kind of man I was to meet with in the poet. Now that I have learned to appreciate his life-philosophy, it seems to me that this is even more noteworthy than his verse. We are all of us engaged, in some way or another, with the problem of co-ordinating the Hellenic and Christian ideals, or, what is much the same thing, of adapting Christian traditions to the governing conceptions of a scientific age. Lefroy proved that it is possible to combine religious faith with frank delight in natural loveliness, to be a Christian without asceticism, and a Greek without sensuality. I can imagine that this will appear simple to many of my readers. They will exclaim : " We do not need a minor poet like Lefroy to teach that lesson. Has not the problem been solved by thousands ?" Perhaps it has. But there is a specific note, a particular purity, a clarified distinction, in the amalgam offered by Lefroy. What I have called his spiritual apperception of sensuous beauty was the outcome of a rare and exquisite personality. It has the translucent quality of a gem, beryl or jacinth, which, turn it to the light and view it from all sides, retains one flawless colour. This simplicity and absolute sincerity of instinct is surely uncommon in our perplexed epoch. To rest for a moment upon the spontaneous and unambitious poetry which flowed from such a nature cannot fail to refresh minds wearied with the storm and stress of modern thought. To abide in communion with an individuality so finely and felicitously moulded must be a source of strength and soothing to those even who find themselves incapable of taking up exactly the same fundamental principles.

LA BÊTE HUMAINE

A STUDY IN ZOLA'S IDEALISM

IT is one of the *mauvaises plaisanteries* of the epoch to call M. Zola a realist. Actually, he is an idealist of the purest water; and if idealists are Philistines, then Gath can claim him for her own. The ponderousness of his method, the tedium of his descriptions, and the indecencies in which he revels, do not justify his claim to stand outside the ranks of those who treat reality from an ideal point of view. Walt Whitman, one of the staunchest idealists who ever uttered prophecy, might be made to pass for a realist on the same grounds of heaviness, minuteness, and indecency. The fact is that Zola, like Whitman, approaches his art-work in the spirit of a poet.

These assertions have an odour of paradox, and require demonstration. That may be supplied by an analysis of "La Bête Humaine." I will call this book the poem of the railway. It is, indeed, a great deal more than that. But the unity of subject, movement, composition, interest, which constitutes a creation of idealising art, and distinguishes that from the haphazard incompleteness of reality, is found by Zola in the biography of an engine on the line between Paris and Havre. "La Lison," as the locomotive is named, might be termed the heroine of the romance.

This unity, which constitutes an ideal creation of the brain, separating that from fact or from any literal transcripts of reality, is sustained with extraordinary ability and constructive genius throughout "La Bête Humaine." All the personages of the drama are in one way or another connected with the company of the Ouest line : as directors, station-masters, guards, engine-drivers, stokers, pointsmen, with their wives and mistresses. The unity of place is equally preserved. Of the many tragic episodes to which the action gives rise, all are prepared at Paris or Havre in buildings attached to the railway stations, and all are consummated at a certain fatal point between the stopping-places of Malaunay and Barentin. There is a tunnel which plays an important part in each catastrophe, and a wayside house of doom at Croix-de-Maufras. This house, in truth, has a right to claim equality with the palace of Atreus at Mycenæ. It is just as mysterious, and no less haunted by the Furies of an ancient crime. Guilty and innocent alike are drawn within its neighbourhood, to be involved in the mesh of destiny, which eventually entangles all the *dramatis personæ*. The scheme by which Zola has worked out this unity of subject, place and retribution is so mathematically perfect, so mechanically exact, as to set all the probabilities of actual events at defiance. Only the extreme vivacity and photographic accuracy of each incident in detail blind us to the immense demand continually made upon our credulity by the poet's ideality.

What is the meaning of the title. We find it in this sentence: "Posséder, tuer, cela s'équivalait-il, dans le fond sombre de la bête humaine?" (p. 196). Murder and sexual desire, co-existent, confounding their qualities, emergent one out of the other, in the nature of the irredeemable wild beast, man : that is the double subject of the book. These two brutal factors persist in humanity. The machinery of modern life, the train which goes hurling and howling down the grooves of progress, remains an idle instrument beside the passions of the human beast. "Ah ! c'est une belle invention, il n'y a pas à dire," says one of the persons in the story: "on va vite, on est plus savant. . . . . Mais les bêtes sauvages restent des bêtes sauvages, et on aura beau inventer des mécaniques meilleures encore, il y aura quand même des bêtes sauvages dessous" (p. 45). That other great invention of the civilised brain, legal justice, fails to solve the problems of social life, cannot penetrate the passions which impel the wild beast, man, to improbable or inconceivable actions. The ineptitude of the judge, M. Denizet, acute and industrious in the search after truth as he may be, forms a moral pendant to the blind brute force of the locomotive which whirls human beings to destruction. Justice does not fathom the profundities of the beast's heart any better than the railway engine is capable of sympathising with its emotions.

The poetic unity which marks *La Bête Humaine* out as a masterpiece of the constructive imagination, cannot be fully appreciated without passing the main actors of its drama in review. The first to whom we are introduced is a man called Roubaud, "sous-chef de gare," or second stationmaster, at Havre. He had risen from the ranks, passing through several grades in the company's service, until his vigour and good conduct prepared him for a higher post. That, however, might have still been long in coming had he not married a young woman called Séverine, who was the protégée of the President Grandmorin, one of the acting directors in the company. Séverine, a daughter of Grandmorin's gardener, had been taken into the great man's family upon the death of her father, and grew up in humble companionship with his only daughter Berthe. Roubaud, now on the verge of forty, wooed and won this girl, his junior by fifteen years. Grandmorin gave her a marriage portion of £400, advanced her husband to the post of station-master, and promised to leave her by his will a house at Croix-de-Maufras, on the line between Rouen and Havre. The property was valued at about £1600.

Séverine is described as one of those graceful fascinating women who charm men without possessing any peculiar beauty. Her great attraction for the rough railway servant was the distinction she derived from her education in Grandmorin's family. Rather tall and slender, she had a wealth of undulating dark hair, framing her pale face, and eyes of clear grey blue—"yeux de pervenche." Roubaud suspected nothing wrong in the protection extended to her by the president ; for though there were disquieting rumours afloat about his conduct, he had reached an advanced if vigorous old age, stood well at the Imperial Court, and owned a property of some three millions of francs.

During the opening scene between husband and wife, which takes place in a little room overlooking the station of the Ouest at Paris, an accident leads Roubaud to the discovery that M. Grandmorin had foully abused his quasi-guardianship of the young woman when she was a girl of sixteen. The wild beast in the man awakes. His first impulse is to murder his wife, and he very nearly does so with fists and feet. On second thoughts, he determines to murder Grandmorin. Opportunity enables him to do so that very evening in a railway carriage between Malaunay and Barentin. The weapon used is a knife which Séverine had just given him. The place selected is the tunnel which has been already mentioned. But the deed had not been completed before the train emerged from the tunnel, and swept on along a hedgerow. At that point lay a young man, who had just time to catch the vision of Roubaud stabbing his victim in the throat, while a mass of something black weighed on the murdered person's legs. He could not, however, remember with any distinctness the features of the two men, and was not certain whether the black mass was a woman or a railway-rug.

It is not necessary to describe how Roubaud's professional familiarity with railway trains enabled him and Séverine to escape detection by shifting from one carriage to another, and back again, at well-chosen moments. Enough that they reached Havre apparently as usual, and though suspected of the crime (their alleged motive being a wish to anticipate Grandmorin's bequest of the house at Croix-de-Maufras), they were finally dismissed without a stain upon their reputations.

The young man who obtained that fleeting vision of the murder is Jacques Lantier, a son of Gervaise (the heroine of Zola's *L'Assommoir*), and brother of a suicidal painter (the hero of Zola's *L'Œuvre*). There is also one of the Lantiers in Zola's *Germinal*. His peculiarity of temperament has to be noticed. Coming of what would now be called a neuropathical stock, he was the victim of an inborn homicidal instinct. It took the special form, that, from the age of dawning manhood, he never desired a woman without at the same time being irresistibly impelled to kill her. "Tuer une femme, tuer une femme! cela sonnait à ses oreilles, du fond de sa jeunesse, avec la fièvre grandissante, affolante du désir. Comme les autres, sous l'éveil de la puberté, rêvent d'en posséder une, lui s'était enragé à l'idée d'en tuer une" (p. 57). A vague impression haunts his brain that this terrible perversion of the sexual instinct derives from a remote ancestry. Sitting by women in the theatre, passing them in the streets, suddenly the insane abominable impulse comes upon him, like a force superior to his will and reason. " Puisqu'il ne les connaissait pas, quelle fureur pouvait-il avoir contre elles ? car, chaque fois, c'était comme une soudaine crise de rage aveugle, une soif toujours renaissante de venger des offenses très anciennes, dont il aurait perdu l'exacte mémoire. Cela venait-il donc de si loin, du mal que les femmes avaient fait à sa race, de la rancune amassée de mâle en mâle, depuis la première tromperie au fond des cavernes ? " For the rest, Jacques Lantier is a young man of more than ordinary refinement ; physically attractive, with well-formed hands and a face that would have been eminently sympathetic but for the restlessness of the brown eyes, shot at times with flakes of red. His position in the railway company, which connects all these people in one sphere of work, is that of engine-driver. Debarred from the society of women by the fearful malady which preys upon his brain, Lantier has made a mistress of his engine, the strong, beautiful, responsive creature, Lison, who twice daily performs the journey between Havre and Paris with express trains.

Lantier found himself in the evening of Grandmorin's murder on the bank above the tunnel's mouth, owing to a series of incidents which must be related. A group of persons highly important to the plot of *La Bête Humaine* appear now upon the stage. Jacques had gone to visit a female cousin of his father, who brought him up at Plassans when his mother Gervaise deserted him at the age of six. This woman, "tante Phasie," as she is called, was left a widow with two daughters, Flore and Louisette. For her second husband she married a miserable, lifeless creature named Misard, who is employed upon the line of the Ouest as signalman, at Croix-de-Maufras. The house inhabited by the Misards stands close to the railway, so that it is shaken by the thunder of all the trains that pass; and at night the glare of their illuminated carriages startles the sleepers in the bedrooms, and leaves upon wakeful brains the silhouettes of countless travellers going and coming upon the iron highway of the world. Close by lies the deserted garden and the empty house which Séverine is destined to inherit from the President Grandmorin. We are, therefore, at the local centre of the tragedy. Misard, the signalman, is actuated by only one motive in life, a slow, persistent avarice. It works in his dull brain like a spreading disease; and just at this moment it has brought him to the commission of a crime. He is poisoning Phasie by little doses introduced into her food, in order to gain possession of some thousand francs which she has recently inherited. The woman knows what her husband has in view. But she fancies herself strong and keen-witted enough to defeat him, and persists in this illusion till she dies of poison on the night which determines one of the great crises of the tragedy.

The two girls, Flore and Louisette, both of them play parts in this closely woven drama. Louisette went out to service in the country house of Grandmorin. One day she left her situation in a miserable plight, telling a dark story of her master's violence, signs of which were only too visible upon her body. Instead of going home to Phasie, she took refuge in the woods with a sort of gentle savage, a veritable Orson, whom she called her " bon ami," and whom in the natural course of events she would probably have married. The name of this man is Cabuche. Endowed with herculean strength, he had killed a man by accident in a tavern brawl, and had been sentenced to five years' penal servitude. Leaving the prison at the end of four years with a good character for discipline and industry, Cabuche found himself avoided by his neighbours, and went off to live in a hut close to some deserted quarries. Here he employed himself in excavating huge blocks of stone and carting them down to the nearest railway station. The pure and intimate relation which sprang up between him and the innocent child Louisette, forms one of those romantic episodes that bloom like flowers upon the arid rock of Zola's human wilderness. Louisette died of fever in the forest hut; and Cabuche, knowing well the real cause of her death, vowed to take the life of Grandmorin. Suspicion naturally fell on him when the president was murdered; and it was only due to political reasons for quashing the whole investigation that the good-hearted giant did not fall a victim to M. Denizet's (the magistrate's) well-reasoned system of analysis. Eventually, by another train of circumstances which illustrates Zola's plot-weaving and dexterous manipulation of his characters, Cabuche is condemned for a murder of which he is equally guiltless. He and Louisette are the victims of fatality, crime in others, the mistakes of justice.

Flore has her own place on the railway. At Croix-de-Maufras, close by Misard's signal-box, there is a level crossing. It is her duty to attend to the opening and shutting of the barriers at this point. Zola has drawn in Flore the portrait of an Amazon, a primeval virgin, a nymph of Dian's train. " Une grande fille de dix-huit ans, blonde, forte, à la bouche épaisse, aux grands yeux verdâtres, au front bas sous de lourds cheveux. Elle n'était point jolie, elle avait les hanches solides et les bras durs d'un garçon" (p. 37). Possessed of enormous physical force, she kept importunate suitors at a distance by the weight of her arms and fists. "Elle était vierge et guerriére, dédaigneuse du mâle, ce qui finissait par convaincre les gens qu'elle avait pour sûr la tête dérangée" (p. 53). The fact is that she had early set her affections upon Jacques Lantier, and was open to no other influence of the passions. On the evening of his visit to "la tante Phasie," chance brought them alone together in the president's deserted garden. The emotional trouble of the girl roused Lantier's latent malady. He was seized with the irresistible impulse to kill instead of possessing this woman on the point of yielding. Rushing from her arms to avoid the horrible suggestion, he roamed in the dark over field and hedge until he sank exhausted at the spot where the vision of Grandmorin's murder flashed across his eyes. The ending of Flore's history may here be related. Seeing Jacques devote himself to another woman, and growing in course of time to hate them both, she determined to wreck an express train which she knew would carry the lovers to Paris on a certain day. Flore attained her object by contriving to arrest Cabuche's waggon with its load of blocks upon the level crossing just before the train came by. The smash, of course, was awful. But Flore had the disappointment of finding that neither Jacques nor his mistress had been killed. He was carried, bruised and wounded, into Grandmorin's house at Croix-de-Maufras. There Séverine, for she was the woman, nursed him, and there he eventually murdered her with the same knife Roubaud had used to stab the president. But this is anticipating the order of events. When Flore saw that she had failed in the main part of her design, and reflected on the number of human lives she had sacrificed—lives hitherto unreckoned by her, since daily cargoes of passengers, unknown, unheeded, had been always going and coming on the wings of steam before her eyes—she walked straight into the tunnel, and standing upright before an approaching train, was shattered to bits by the iron cuirass of the engine. They laid what was left of her mangled form by the side of her mother Phasie, who was lying dead of Misard's poison in the signalman's house.

Up to the present point of the analysis we have had several types of murderers presented to us. There is Roubaud, who kills from motives of revenge and retrospective jealousy ; Misard, who poisons his wife to get her money ; Cabuche, who commits an accidental homicide through heat of blood and strength of muscle ; Lantier, who is the subject of a perverted instinct, changing the natural impulse of sex into blood-lust; Flore, whose jealousy prompts her to sacrifice a hecatomb of human victims in the hope of killing her lover and her rival; Grandmorin, whose abnormal vices in old age lead to the death of innocent Louisette. There remains one other personage necessary to the unity of this remarkable plot. He is Lantier's stoker, a debauched drunkard, called Pecqueux, who works in good relations with the engine-driver on their common pet, la Lison. Poor Lison, by the way, ends her own locomotive life in the wreck of the train at Croix-de-Maufras. Lantier and Pecqueux have to drive another, and do so with their usual harmony until Pecqueux obtains ocular evidence that Lantier has been tampering with his mistress Philomène. Of Philomène, one of Zola's disagreeable characters, it is only necessary to say that she lives in the station at Havre, keeping house for her brother, the "chef de dépôt," and pursuing a course of reckless immorality. Lantier was never in any true sense her lover. But the stoker's jealousy once roused he determines to revenge himself. It happens, accordingly, that being more drunk than usual one day he refuses to obey the engine-driver's orders and insults him. They are alone together on their locomotive, carrying a trainful of soldiers, packed in cattle-pens, to Paris; for the Franco-Prussian War has broken out, troops are being concentrated, and these men will be drafted from Paris to the frontier. The quarrel begun by Pecqueux ends in a struggle for supremacy between the two men, in the course of which both fall from the engine and are killed upon the spot. *La Bête Humaine* winds up with a description of the train and its freight of soldiers hurling along the rails, dashing through stations, driverless, uncontrollable. In what I have called the idealism of Zola, this termination of the story with its prospect of carnage and the vision of man's mechanical instrument let loose upon the pathway of destruction is highly dramatic. He closes *Nana* with the shouts of the Parisians yelling, "À Berlin!" The whole series of the Rougon-Macquart volumes lead up to the fall of the Empire. Again, with special reference to this particular romance, the crowding together of a mass of human animals, soldiers, food for powder, who are launched into eternity through the jealous fury of a drunken homicide—nothing, I assert, could be better arranged to sustain the central idea, or less probable as a piece of fortuitous reality. It also has to be remarked that Pecqueux's fatal quarrel begins at Croix-de-Maufras, which I have called the local centre of the tragic drama. Dante himself could not have designed the machinery of a poem with more mathematical precision than Zola has displayed in the construction of this plot. Nature and the course of events, it need hardly be said, do not act in this way.

Before proceeding to draw final critical conclusions, I have to resume what, after all, is the most interesting matter in the book—Lantier's love-affair with Séverine. We have seen how the engine-driver had a vision of the murder of Grandmorin in the railway-carriage. Called as a witness, he made a clean breast of all he knew, but positively declared his inability to identify any of the accused persons. Still he became naturally an object of great anxiety to the Roubauds; and their strange behaviour toward him, displayed in petty acts of courtesy and signs of curiosity, convinced him that Roubaud was the murderer, and that the black mass he had discerned so dimly was the body of Séverine. The three persons came thus to be drawn together in a complicity of knowledge, though they never discussed the details of the crime. Roubaud almost pushed Lantier into his wife's arms; and Lantier found, to his great astonishment, that he could love her without awakening the homicidal demon in his breast. The very fact that she was a murderess seemed to render her inviolable. Séverine, yielding by slow degrees to the young man's passion, discerned for the first time what it was to love with the heart. Her previous relations with Grandmorin and Roubaud had not aroused the woman in her. Lantier's delicate attentions, the difficulties of the situation, and finally the rapture of possession, made her his slave. She grew to hate her husband, who, since the epoch of the murder, abandoned himself wholly to the vice of gaming. Then she prompted her lover to kill the man who stood in the way of their union. But Lantier, in spite of his peculiar homicidal insanity, could not murder in cold blood. At last they agreed to decoy Roubaud alone one evening to the empty house at Croix-de-Maufras, and there Lantier promised he would do the deed. The knife which had stabbed Grandmorin was ready on the table. However, just at the fatal moment, certain imprudences of Séverine brought a paroxysm of his malady upon her lover. Lantier thrust the knife of destiny into her throat, at the very point on the railway where Grandmorin received his death-blow, and in the room where Grandmorin's crime with her had been committed so many years ago. He escaped unseen, leaving the house-door open ; and when Roubaud arrived with Misard, they found the unfortunate Cabuche there covered with Séverine's blood. The presence of Cabuche is well *motivirt* (as Goethe would say); and accessory circumstances lead M. Denizet to the conclusion that he was the murderer of both Grandmorin and Séverine, instigated in each case by Roubaud. During the course of the judicial proceedings Roubaud confesses the murder of the president, and is condemned. Cabuche has to bear the guilt of Séverine's assassination.

This analysis of *La Bête Humaine* shows in how true a sense it may be called a poem. It has all those qualities of the constructive reason by which an ideal is distinguished from the bare reality. Not only does it violate our sense of probability in life that ten persons should be either murderers or murdered, or both together, when all of them exist in close relations through their common connection with one line of railway, but the short space of time required for the evolution of this intricate drama of blood and appetite is also unnatural. Eighteen months suffice for the unfolding and termination of the whole series of homicidal tragedies. At the end, the stage is swept literally bare by the violent deaths of all the principal persons who played their parts upon it, with the exception of Misard, who marries a woman of bad character, Roubaud, who goes to life-imprisonment, and the unfortunate Cabuche, who receives a similar doom. Even la Lison is destroyed, and her successor is consigned to probable perdition by the insane fury of Pecqueux. Nor is this all. The conditions of place are manipulated with equal idealistic ingenuity. I have already pointed out how all the threads of the drama are tied together in one knot at Croix-de-Maufras, that place upon the line between Malaunay and Barentin at the entrance to the fatal tunnel. When Lantier comes to the president's deserted house, at the commencement of the story, he regards it with a superstitious dread. "Cette maison, il la connaissait bien, il la regardait à chacun de ses voyages, dans le branle grondant de la machine. Elle le hantait sans qu'il sût pourquoi, avec la sensation confuse qu'elle importait à son existence" (p. 51). It was here that he fled from Flore under one access of his homicidal mania, and it was here that he murdered Séverine under the pressure of another. Here Grandmorin had previously corrupted the girlhood of Madame Roubaud. In its close vicinity stood the house where Madame Misard died of poison, hard by the level crossing where Flore wrecked the train, not far from the tunnel where Grandmorin was stabbed, Flore committed suicide, and Pecqueux made his slaughterous attack on Lantier. Nor must we forget the fatal knife, that present which Séverine gave her husband in the opening scene, which he used to assassinate the president, which Séverine meant should be the instrument of Roubaud's death, and which Lantier finally plunged into her own throat. It is impossible to contend that this interweaving of a numerous *dramatis personæ* in one mesh of homicidal crime, this concentration of so many murderous incidents upon one spot, this crowding of them into less than two years, and this part played by the fatal knife, are realistic—if realism means a faithful correspondence to facts as we observe them, and a reproduction of the events of life as they are known to us.

It may be urged that not a single character, or motive, or circumstance in the whole prose-poem (a long poem of four hundred and fifteen closely-printed pages) has been idealised. That is quite true. The people are studied from life. They act and talk naturally. They say and do a large number of things which are usually concealed in literature, but which are none the less veracious. The mechanism and management of a great main line in France have been reproduced with carefully accumulated details which we may assume to be exact. Few of M. Zola's critics know as much about such things as he does. Also, the conduct of a train, its composition, the relations of guards, station-masters, engine-drivers, stokers, pointsmen, to one another, to the machine they set in motion and control, and to the passengers they carry, are presented with Zola's usual detail, and with more than his usual feeling for the poetry inherent in this phase of modern life. The only point for criticism is at the end of the romance, when the train, with its freight of military cattle, starts forth driverless upon that terrific course. Here we might, indeed, pause to wonder how long the engine would speed on alone with no one to stoke up its furnace. Here, and here perhaps for once, M. Zola yields consciously to the incorrigible idealism of an artist. The romance closes with the prospect of a tragedy which fitly winds the poem up, but which might very probably have failed for want of coals.

Zola's realism consists, then, in his careful attention to details, in the naturalness of his connecting motives, and his frank acceptance of all things human which present themselves to his observing brain. The idealism which I have been insisting on, which justifies us in calling *La Bête Humaine* a poem, has to be sought in the method whereby these separate parcels of the plot are woven together, and also in the dominating conception contained in the title which gives unity to the whole work. We are not in the real region of reality, but in the region of the constructive imagination from the first to the last line of the novel. If that be not the essence of idealism—this working of the artist's brain not in but on the subject-matter of the external world and human nature—I do not know what meaning to give to the term.

MEDIÆVAL NORMAN SONGS

VAL DE VIRE was one of the richest and most favoured regions of old Normandy. The country has a look of Devonshire or Somerset. Grassland and orchards intersected by deep lanes, feathery with ferns and fox-gloves. Sluggish streams, bordered with yellow flags and flowering rush; banks blue with columbine. Spinneys and copses, mossy homesteads, hedged grazing meadows, humble churches, slouching stablemen, and sturdy farmers. The names of towns and villages remind one constantly of noble English families, who came from them across the channel, and of these one of the most picturesquely situated is St. Lo. It stands on a hill of solid grey rock overhanging the Vire—a stream not unlike our Avon, which winds through wooded slopes of dark red iron-stone and lime-stone, curving a gentle course toward the open plain and not far distant sea. The valley, the river, the woods, the gardens on the hills, the broad meadow-land beyond, can all be surveyed from the square of the Cathedral. This is an irregular and decrepit old church, interesting by reason of its imperfections. No one part of the building corresponds to the rest; the chapels sprawl at oblique angles; the towers are ingeniously constructed to combine similarity and difference. The workmanship throughout is loose, dishevelled, mongrel. Yet there are beautiful wide windows: labyrinths of grey glass, like spiders' webs, enclosing figures bright as gems with green and blue and fiery crimson. Outside, there is a little stone pulpit—like the one in the courtyard of Magdalen College Oxford—open to the air, with a Gothic canopy above it. Here one can fancy monks preaching or pardoners displaying their indulgences to country folk in Lent.

It was at St. Lo that I picked up a collection of "Chansons Normandes du xvme Siècle," published from manuscripts existing in private libraries at Vire and Bayeux. They consist for the most part of drinking-songs and love-ditties; but fragments of ballads and a few patriotic songs, relating to the wars with England, give variety to this material. Like all literary efforts of a rustic population, the Vaux de Vire, as they were called, are distinguished by simplicity and spontaneity. Their frequent repetition of the same ideas proves the intellectual poverty of the source from which they were derived. The want of art in their composition guarantees the genuineness of the feelings which produced them. We seem, while reading their refrains and lays, to hear the voices of generations living tranquilly in the same round, revolving in one routine of natural joys and sorrows : rejoicing in the warmth of summer, and shrinking from the winter's cold ; expanding in the spring to love, and welcoming the autumn with its gift of wine and fruit. There is a pathos in this half-developed poetry, like that which thrills us in the unfoldings of the first buds and leaves of spring. It is so near to all things natural ; like earth herself, so very old and yet so fresh and new. Centuries and centuries of men and women have felt and sung like this : used the same images of joy adopted from the fields in April or in May, crooned the same melodies borrowed from streams and winds and waving trees. The song of the thrush and the blackbird, the note of the nightingale, the blossoms of the apple-tree and thorn, the freshness of the greenwood after winter snows have melted— these are the ever recurring themes of pleasure, hope, and love, on which the rustic singers dwell. It is a poetry singularly sympathetic to the pastoral country which developed it. The lyrics of the Minnesingers and Provençal Troubadours have something similar in monotone to this; but the clang of arms and the stirring of the great world were never far distant from the ladies' bowers in which they sounded: whereas these Norman ditties breathe of nothing but the crofts and cottages and pastures of a village. If the noise of war is heard at all in Val de Vire, it is but some marauding band of English foragers, who come to lift the cattle and to make great pillage of the Duchy. The peasants rise and do their best to pay back force with force, and deep and deadly is the hatred stored against their foes. From the beginning to the end of this scanty literature, we remain within the narrow circle of local interests, and it is this which gives it a peculiar charm. The Vaux de Vire should be read in Normandy in May. Their flavour, like that of the cider which gushes from the presses of St. Lo or St. Sever, is native to the fat fair orchard-land which gave them birth so many years ago.

To translate popular songs is never very easy. Yet these offer fewer difficulties than those, for instance, of the Tuscan and the Umbrian highlands. The old French is clear and limpid; the metrical structure in most cases very simple. It will be observed that, in the English versions I am about to offer, one peculiarity of the originals —a curious monotony of recurring and repeated rhymes—has been retained. The succession of rhymes I have sometimes altered, where I thought our language needed it.

The first group are the love-songs, by far the most numerous and characteristic of the collection. We may start with one in which a lover sings the praises of his sweetheart:

> *Fair is her body, bright her eye,*
> *With smiles her mouth is kind to me;*
> *Then, think no evil, this is she*
> *Whom God hath made my only joy.*
>
> *Between the earth and heaven high*
> *There is no maid so fair as she;*
> *The beauty of her sweet body*
> *Doth ever fill my heart with joy.*
>
> *He is a knave, nor do I lie,*
> *Who loveth her not heartily;*
> *The grace that shines from her body*
> *Giveth to lovers all great joy.*

Sometimes the accented passages remind us of Elizabethan lyric, as in the repeated last line of the following quatrain:

> *Sad, lost in thought, and mute I go:*
> *The cause, ah me! you know full well:*
> *But see that nought thereof you tell,*
> *For men will only laugh at woe—*
> *For men will only laugh at woe.*

The same effect is gained by the echoed questions in this catch:

> *Kiss me then, my merry May,*
> *By the soul of love I pray!*
>   *Prithee, nay! Tell, tell me why?*
> *If with you I sport and play,*
> *My mother will be vexed to-day.*
>   *Tell me why, oh, tell me why?*

I must confess to having slightly modernised two pretty but imperfect pieces, which play upon the different tribes of singing birds:

> *Before my lady's window gay,*
> *The little birds they sing all day,*
>   *The lark, the mavis, and the dove;*
> *But the sweet nightingale of May,*
> *She whiles the silent hours away,*
>   *Chanting of sorrow, joy, and love.*

The dove in the next song is clearly metaphorical for some fair damsel, who has been tamed to appreciate the caresses of a swain:

> *I found at daybreak yester morn,*
> *Close by the nest where she was born,*
>   *A tender turtle dove:*
> *Oha! ohé! ohesa, hesa, hé!*
>
> *She fluttered, but she could not fly;*
> *I heard, but would not heed her cry:*
>   *She had not learned to love:*
> *Oha! ohé! ohesa, hesa, hé!*

> *Now she is quiet on my breast,*
> *And from her new and living nest*
> *She doth not seek to rove:*
> *Oha! ohé! ohesa, hesa, hé!*

Occasionally the lyric note closely resembles that belonging to the love-songs of the Carmina Burana. I have found, in translating both, that the effect produced in English is almost exactly the same, without any intention on my own part. This is the case with the rather pretty but insipid piece which follows:

> *This month of May, one pleasant eventide,*
> *I heard a young girl singing on the green;*
> *I came upon her where the ways divide,*
> *And said, " God keep you, maiden, from all teen.*
>
> *" Maiden, the God of love you keep and save,*
> *And give you all your heart desires," I cried.*
> *Then she: " Pray tell me, gentle sir and brave,*
> *Whither you wend this pleasant eventide?"*
>
> *" To you I come, a lover leal and true,*
> *To tell you all my hope and all my care;*
> *Your love alone is what I seek; than you*
> *No woman ever seemed to me more fair."*

The parting of two lovers, also in the leafy forest-glades, has a throb of keener passion:

> *In this first merry morn of May,*
> *When as the year grows young and green,*
> *Into the wood I went my way,*
> *To say farewell unto my queen.*

> *And when we could no longer stay,*
> *Weeping upon my neck she fell,*
> *Oh, send me news from far away!*
> *Farewell, sweet heart of mine, farewell!*

The ladies, in the absence of their lovers, are anxious for news. Their longing thoughts do not, however, borrow the wings of a bird, as in the more imaginative poetry of central Italy. The heart's unrest finds simpler expression. Take for instance the following song, the close of which strikes me as charmingly fanciful in its disconnection from the main theme :

> *O Love, my love and perfect bliss!*
> *God in His goodness grant me this—*
>   *I see thee soon again.*
> *Nought else I need to take away*
> *The grief that for thy sake alway*
>   *Doth keep me in great pain.*
>
> *Alas! I know not what to do,*
> *Nor how to get good news and true:*
>   *Dear God, I pray to Thee;*
> *If else Thou canst not comfort me,*
> *Of Thy great mercy make that he*
>   *Send speedy news to me.*
>
> *Within my father's garden walls*
> *There is a tree—when April falls*
>   *It blossometh alway.*
> *There wend I oft in winter drear,*
> *Yea, and in spring, the winds to hear,*
>   *The sweet winds at their play.*

The motif of a bird as messenger occurs in the next ditty; but a nightingale, and not the swallow, has been chosen:

Alas! poor heart, I pity thee
For all the grief thou hast and care!
My love I see not anywhere;
He is so far away from me.

Until once more his face I see
I shall be sad by night and day;
And if his face I may not see
Then I shall die most certainly:
For other pleasures have I none,
And all my hope is this alone.
   No ease I take by night and day:
   O Love, my love, to thee I pray
        Have pity upon me!

Dear nightingale of woodland gay,
   Who singest on the leafy tree,
Go, take a message I thee pray,
   A message to my love from me;
Tell, tell him that I waste away
And weaker grow from day to day.

Ah, God! what pain and grief have we
   Who are poor lovers, leal and true:
   For every week that we pass through,
Five hundred thousand griefs have we:
   One cannot think, or count, or tell
   The griefs and pains that we know well!

A forlorn swain echoes the same lament in stanzas which, though monotonous, have an accent of poignant sincerity :

> *Now who is he on earth that lives,*
>   *Who knows or with his tongue can say*
> *What grief to poor lovers it gives*
>   *To love with loyal heart alway?*
>
> *So bitter is their portion, yea,*
>   *So hard their part!*
> *But this doth more confound my heart;*
> *Unloved to love, and still to pray!*
> *Thinking thereon I swoon away.*

A man is trying to unlock the secret of a maiden's bosom. It is a lover and his lass, sauntering in twilight between hedgerows heavy with the scent of honeysuckle and wild roses. From the tenour of the swain's pleading, we may feel assured that he does not suffer under any great anxiety about her answer :

> *Sweet flower, that art so fair and gay,*
>   *Come tell me if thou lovest me!*
> *Think well, and tell me presently:*
> *For sore it irks me, by my fay,*
>
> *For sore it irketh me alway,*
>   *That I know not the mind of thee:*
> *I pray thee, gentle lady gay,*
>   *If so thou wilt, tell truth to me.*

> *For I do love thee so, sweet May,*
> *That if my heart thou wert to see,*
> *In sooth I know, of courtesy,*
> *Thou wouldst have pity on me this day.*

A girl has plighted her troth. She is sure of the man's loyalty, tranquil in the sense of his affection; not to repay him with truth and kindness in like measure, would be base:

> *My love for him shall be*
> *Fair love and true:*
> *For he loves me, I know,*
> *And I love him, pardie!*
>
> *And for I know that he,*
> *Doth love me so,*
> *I should be all untrue*
> *To love but him, pardie!*

The greenwood was the common trysting place for sweethearts. Here is a song of spring-time in which the contentment of secure affection is very prettily expressed:

> *Beneath the branch of the green may*
> *My merry heart sleeps happily,*
> *Waiting for him who promised me*
> *To meet me here again this day.*
>
> *And what is that I would not do*
> *To please my love so dear to me?*
> *He loves me with leal heart and true,*
> *And I love him no less, pardie!*

> *Perchance I see him but a day;*
> *Yet maketh he my heart so free—*
> *His beauty so rejoiceth me—*
> *That months thereafter I am gay.*

We hear a good deal about "faux jaloux" and scandals, calumnious reports, and malignant gossip. A damsel is indignant because her sweetheart's personal appearance has been depreciated by persons who might have been better occupied in minding their own business:

> *They have said evil of my dear;*
> *Therefore my heart is vexed and drear:*
>   *But what is it to them*
> *If he be fair or foul to see,*
> *Since he is perfect joy to me.*
>
> *He loves me well: the like do I:*
> *I do not look with half an eye,*
>   *But seek to pleasure him.*
>
> *From all the rest I choose him here;*
> *I want no other for my dear:*
>   *How then should he displease*
> *Those who may leave him if they please?*
>   *God keep him from all fear!*

A stormier burst of indignation escapes from the lips of a man who has been slandered to his mistress. This lyric, in pure literary quality, is one of the best of the collection:

*They lied, those lying traitors all,
Disloyal, hypocritical,
  Who feigned that I spake ill of thee!
  Heed not their words of charity;
For they are flatterers tongued with gall,
  And liars all.*

*They make the tales that they let fall,
Coining falsehoods, wherewithal
  They swear that I spake ill of thee:
  Heed not their lies of charity;
For they are flatterers tongued with gall,
  And liars all.*

*Believe them not, although they call
Themselves thy servants; one and all,
  They lie, or God's curse light on me!—
  Whatever oaths they swear to thee,
Or were they thrice as stout and tall,
  They're liars all!*

After quoting two stanzas of another song, it will be time to quit these ditties of the spring and love :

*O nightingale of woodland gay,
  Go to my love and to her tell
  That I do love her passing well;
And bid her also think of me,
For I to her will bring the may.*

*The may that I shall bring will be,
  Nor rose nor any opening flower;
  But with my heart I will her dower;
And kisses on her lips I'll lay,
And pray God keep her heartily.*

I can only find one true ballad, in our sense of the word, among these songs. It refers to some tradition about a girl whose sweetheart was a prisoner in her father's castle, and who died when he was brought forth to be hanged.

> Maid Marjory sits at the castle gate:
> With groans and sighs
> She weeps and cries:
> Her grief it is great.
> Her father asks, "Daughter, what is your woe?
> Seek you a husband or lord I trow?"
> "Let husbands be!
> Give my love to me,
> Who pines in the dungeon dark below!"
>
> "I' faith, my daughter, thou'lt long want him;
> For he hangs to-morrow when dawn is dim."
>
> "Then bury my corpse at the gallows' feet;
> And men will say, they were true lovers sweet."

The raciest of these Norman songs are drinking-catches. I find, however, that the lightest and best of them are untranslateable. The delicacy of the French refrains cannot be preserved; the sound of laughter in their facile lines escapes; the gossamer-thread of sense, so lightly spun, is loosened. One satire upon female topers admits of rendering into English. It is curious artistically, by reason of its pertinacious monotony in rhyming. As a picture of manners one may compare it with the scene of Noah's wife and her gossips in the Miracle plays. Similar lyrics occur in Provençal and early Italian poetry. But I think the finest specimen of the type is this:

> *Drink, gossips mine! we drink no wine.*
> *They were three wives that had one heart for wine;*
> *One to the other said—We drink no wine!*
> *Drink, gossips mine! we drink no wine.*
>
> *Drink, gossips mine! we drink no wine.*
> *The varlet stood in jerkin tight and fine*
> *To serve the dames with service of good wine.*
> *Drink, gossips mine! we drink no wine.*
>
> *Drink, gossips mine! we drink no wine.*
> *These wives they cried—Here's service of good wine!*
> *Make we good cheer, nor stint our souls of wine!*
> *Drink, gossips mine! we drink no wine.*
>
> *Drink, gossips mine! we drink no wine.*
> *The gallant fills, nor seeketh further sign,*
> *But crowns the cups with service of good wine.*
> *Drink, gossips mine! we drink no wine.*
>
> *Drink, gossips mine! we drink no wine.*
> *Singing beginneth, and sweet notes combine*
> *With joyance to proclaim the praise of wine!*
> *Drink, gossips mine! we drink no wine.*
>
> *Drink, gossips mine! we drink no wine.*
> *For fear of husbands will we never pine;*
> *They are not here to mar the taste of wine.*
> *Drink, gossips mine! we drink no wine.*

What sort of songs were sung at these convivial meetings appears from another Bacchic melody which follows:—

> *Sweet comrades, fellows of the vine!*
> *Drink we by morn and eve, drink wine—*
> *A cask or so;*
> *Ha, ho!*
> *Nor will we pay our host one jot,*
> *Save a credo!*
>
> *But if our host sue us therefor,*
> *We'll tell him he must pass it o'er*
> *Quasimodo:*
> *Ha, ho!*
> *Nor will we pay our host one jot,*
> *Save a credo!*

The jolliest of all the topers of the Val de Vire was Oliver Basselin, who lived in the reign of Louis XII., and was killed by the English. The song which follows alludes to his death, and to the sadness which it cast over the pleasant company of Vire:—

> *Alas! good Oliver Basselin!*
> *Shall we of you no more hear tell?*
> *And have the English killed you then?*
>
> *You once were wont to sing your songs*
> *And live, I ween, right joyously,*
> *Joining in all the jolly throngs*
> *Throughout the land of Normandy.*

MEDIÆVAL NORMAN SONGS

Far as St. Lo in Cotentin,
Mid fellows fair, as I hear tell,
No pilgrim like to him was seen.

The English they have done great wrong
Unto the fellows of Vau de Vire;
No more shall you hear voice or song
From those who once sang all the year.

To God with stout heart pray we will,
And to Queen Mary, that sweet maid,
To bring the English to all ill:
The Father's curse on them be laid.

The animosity against the English bursts out with even a fiercer growl of rage in some ballads composed expressly upon the ravages inflicted by Henry V.'s soldiery. One patriotic song, with a fine rolling lilt in the line, refers to the death of the hero of Agincourt, and also to the siege of Harfleur, after which Henry expelled the Norman inhabitants and planted in their stead an Anglo-Saxon colony. It further commemorates the exploits of Captain Prégent de Bidoulx, commander of the French warships in 1513, who defended the coast of Normandy from British invaders. Allusion is made in line 7 to the English custom of wearing the hair long, and the name Godar or Godan in line 12 appears to be a corruption of Goddam, the traditional French appellation of an Englishman:

> The English king himself of late let call
> The king of France by style and proclamation:
> His cursèd will it was to summon all
> Good Frenchmen forth from out their land and
>   nation.
> Now is he dead at St. Fiacre en Brie:
> From land of France the churls are ousted quite;
> There sneaks no English pig-tailed cur in sight:
> Cursed be their race and lineage all, say we.
>
> They shipped their battle all upon the sea,
> With store of biscuit and each knave a can;
> And so by sea to Biscay merrily
> Sailed they to crown their little king Godan.
> But all their doing was but idle play,
> So well hath Captain Prégent made them skip;
> Foundered they are by land and eke on ship:
> Cursed by their race and lineage all, say we.

The next has been called the Marseillaise of the Norman peasantry. Even in the original it does not deserve so high-sounding a title, yet the stanzas are interesting for their rustic flavour and for the touches of unconscious humour, which season the deadly hatred they express:—

> Good folk of village, thorp, and hall,
> Who love the French king well,
> Take heart of courage, each and all,
> To fight the English fell.

Seize each his pruning-hook and hoe
  To top them root and branch;
And if you cannot make them go,
  Shew a sour countenance.

Fear not to grapple with them close,
  These Goddams, guts of grease;
For one of us for four of those,
  Or three, is match with ease.

By God, if I could clutch them here—
  And by this oath I stand—
I'd shew them, without feint or fear,
  How heavy is my hand.

Nor pig nor goose in all the shire
  Have they left far or wide:
Nor fowl nor fowl-house by the byre—
  God send them evil tide!

Another ballad, complaining, in like rustic fashion, of oppression and extortion, may possibly refer to English rapine, but more likely to the rapacity of feudal bailiffs and tax-collectors. Commentators differ about the "*court vestus*" in line 9.

In the Duchy of Normandy
Pillage reigns and thievery;
  Of wealth and goods there is no store:
God grant us respite presently,
Or each man, as he may, must flee,
  And leave his home for evermore.

As for me, I will not stay;
  For there is left nor ease nor cheer,
By reason of the shortcoats; they
  Too often come my door anear.

The knaves, with foul discourtesy,
Ask us to give when nought have we,
  And eke they cudgel us full sore:
Nathless, what boots it but that we
Should pray, "Good sirs, of charity,
  Take all we have! What have we more?

Right willingly would I pay toll
  If aught I had wherewith to pay,
But all my wealth, upon my soul,
  And all my goods, are given away.

I cannot show them courtesy
By reason of grim penury,
  Which keepeth me a bondman poor:
Nor friend nor lover dear have I
In France nor yet in Normandy
  To aid with alms my beggared store.

God grant that peace and law might sway
  Through Christendom on every side;
Yea, grant us peace to last alway;
  So might we all secure abide.

If Christendom at one might be,
Then should we live right joyously,
  And shut on grief the prison door:
God curse them who make woes to be,
And eke the blesséd Maid Mary,
  Withouten hope for evermore.

I will add the full title of the volume to which I am indebted for the songs I have translated. It is "Chansons Normandes du xvme siècle, publiées pour la Iere fois sur les manuscrits de Bayeux et de Vire avec introduction et notes de A. Gaste. Caen: Le Gost-Clerisse, Rue Ecuyère 36. 1866."

CLIFTON AND A LAD'S LOVE

Far away in the valley the wind raved; and ever and anon it lashed the panes, whirling up powdery sleet, or bellowed in the chimney. All the middle space of sky had been swept bare by the hurricane. A net of vapour hid the moon, through which she cast a glaring blurred light upon the frozen scene. Beneath lay the city, as clear as in daytime. The church-towers black against the garish snow—their tops and the roof of every house piled with snow, while the dark fronts of buildings traced the course of street and quay and winding river. Far beyond, the hills stood tall and white and spectral, divided by the black lines of their hedgerows. As I gazed, they seemed in that turmoil of tempest to shiver and grow taller and then shrink again, and again to move toward me from their basements. Down there in the town a myriad of twinkling gusty lamps danced and flickered like stars upon a frosty night, except that their light was redder. Our cypresses and tulip-trees and beeches kept grinding and clanging at every wrench of the blast; and sometimes a bough, all bare and dry, was whirled across the window-panes and carried far into the darkness, to be embedded in some distant snow-wreath. All this commotion suggested no thrill of life, no passion. The stolid, pale-faced, blear-eyed heavens and earth seemed lashed by a vindictive fury of dead impersonal force. How different was this from the same landscape last July! Then, after a sleepless night, I rose to watch the dawn between three and four o'clock. Golden light flooded the eastern hills, and came gloriously falling on my bedroom walls, as though the sun were rising for me alone. For there was an almost awful stillness, through which the messenger of day arrived. The birds who had been chirping since the darkness of the dawn, were hushed. No sound of human step or wheel or rustling tree disturbed the silence—nothing but the Cathedral clock striking a half-hour. Domed thunder-clouds, sheeted with gold around their moulded edges, went sailing ponderously eastward, and amber ripplings glimmered beneath them from the water amid those many masts of ships between the houses. These movements of the travelling clouds and sparkling river alone suggested activity, and life was barely indicated by smoke curling from three glass-houses. There I knew that the fires had been kept awake all night by watchers, who listened to the roar of the black chimneys, crying like myself, "Would God that it were morning!"

I

He was all beautiful: as fair
As summer in the silent trees;
As bright as sunshine on the leas;
As gentle as the evening air.

His voice was swifter than the lark;
Softer than thistle-down his cheek;
His eyes were stars that shyly break
At sundown ere the skies are dark.

I found him in a lowly place:
He sang clear songs that made me weep:
Long nights he ruled my soul in sleep:
Long days I thought upon his face.

II

"Alone: and must it then be so?
Why do you walk alone?" she cried.
I answered with a smile, to hide
The undercurrent of my woe.

But had she known, dear friend, that thou
Art living still, she would have said:
"Oblivion should but shroud the dead;
Go, throw thy arms around him now!"

Then on my lips the smile had died:
"From deep to deeper depths I sink;
They bade me leave him on the brink,
And now hell's gulfs our paths divide."

III

This time it is no dream that stirs
The ancient fever of my brain:
The burning pulses throb again,
The thirst I may not quench recurs.

In vain I tell my beating heart
How poor and worthless were the prize:
The stifled wish within me dies,
But leaves an unextinguished smart.

It is not for the love of God
That I have done my soul this wrong;
'Tis not to make my reason strong
Or curb the currents of my blood.

But sloth, and fear of men, and shame
Impose their limit on my bliss:
Else had I laid my lips to his,
And called him by love's dearest name.

I walked with friends to the wood of Druid Stoke. The clouds were like alabaster in the windless sky; sunlight pouring from them with mild intensity and silvery clearness. There we found snowdrops, tall, delicate, and white, among mosses and green ivy. The corymbs of the ivy on those walls of oolite are still ripe, fit to crown fervid brows of amber-skinned Dionysus. The little stream which threads that wood was swollen with rain, and went brawling between grassy banks through cresses with a pretty childish babble. On the fir-trees by the road to Sea-Mills rested very golden light; and there we found red jew's-ears in the hedges. Emerging from the wood into the lowland by the Avon was like passing bodily into a mellow picture by some Dutch painter. The landscape gradually gained in breadth, and when we reached the towing-path, there were for us far-reaching intimations of the sea. Seaweed clings to bits of rock, close beneath oak-boughs and ivy roots, which go creeping downwards to tide-level, and meet the fucus sent up from the sea to seed and grow there. Woodland and wave kiss one another strangely in the peace of those inflowing and receding brackish waters. As we travelled homewards, what wealth of gold and fire and crimson was there abroad on rocks and trees and clouds, what azure of the sky, cloven by those radiant cliffs! Dundry, far away, that long, low, undulating line of hill, stood clear with snow. Steamers splashed panting up and down, fretting a mimic sea. When at length we climbed to Durdham Down, there lay outspread before us glory beyond all glory. Eastward, a mountain range of cloud, stationary, based on blue foundations, towering through all gradations of purple valleys, of crimsoned alps, of golden lights contrasted with pink shadows on ascending ridges, up to one crowning pinnacle of purest snow. In the west rose a jagged castle-wall, fringed with flame, broken with a breach through which the last rays shot ineffable radiance into calm green spaces of the sky, and smote pavilions of frail floating clouds above. All this sky-scape was cloud—cloud such as I have rarely seen, so steeped in colour, so fantastical in shape, so majestic in proportions.

IV

The gale is up, and far away
It comes o'er changeful sea and sand,
Where that dim distant borderland
Stands clear and doffs her mist to-day.

The broad brown woods are close to view;
Their crests are fringed with orange sky,
And here a beech all russet dry,
And here a black rock-pluming yew.

The river swirls with muddy flow;
The wild white sea-gulls screaming sail
Round point and headland on the gale,
Down to the channel's golden glow.

Far up in air the homeward rooks
Float dense against the liquid sky:
They hear the woods beneath them cry,
They mark the swelling of the brooks.

Faint heart, why sad? They flout the breeze,
They care not though their nests be torn;
They laugh the drenching showers to scorn:
Wilt thou not wing thy way like these?

V

The chimes upon this troubled air
Went sighing, sobbing to the night.
Day drew the curtain from the light,
And left the new year bleak and bare.

A heaven inpenetrably black;
Earth sullen, hard, and well defined:
No hope above; the clouds are blind,
And from the East fast whirls the wrack.

VI

The stately ships are passing free,
Where scant light strikes along the flood;
Gaunt winter scowls o'er field and wood?
O who will bring my love to me?

L

White gulls fly screaming to the sea;
The bitter east wind sweeps the sky;
Faint snow streaks on the hill-sides lie:
O who will bring my love to me?

The hawthorn bough is bare and dree;
The spiky holly keeps him warm;
Brown brake shrills shivering in the storm:
O who will bring my love to me?

The bright blue sky is cold to see;
The frosty ground lies hard and bare;
So cold is hope, so hard is care:
O who will bring my love to me?

Low on the horizon, beyond Durdham Down, were streaks of white light, wavering spokes and flaring lines and streamers, flushing into faint rose-pink. Could the buried sunlight still be felt so late into a night of May? Soon, by quiverings and motions in these signs—for the west darkened, and flames burst forth among the topmost stars, and toward the east ran swords, stealthily creeping across the heavenly spaces—I knew that this was an Aurora Borealis. The pageant rapidly developed, and culminated with dramatic vividness. At the very zenith, curving downward to the Great Bear, there shone a nebulous semi-circle—phosphorescent, with stars tangled in it. From this crescent of light were effused to north and west and east rays, bands, foam-flakes, belts, spears, shafts of changeful hues, now rosy red, now brightening into amethyst, now green, now pale as ashes. The whole was in slow and solemn movement, like lightning congealed, which has not ceased to throb. As glaciers are to running water, so were these auroral flames to the quiverings of lightning. In the midst of all the glow and glory sparkled Ursa Major, calm and frosty. Other stars seemed to wander in the haze, as I have seen them in a comet's tail. The most wonderful point in the pageant was when the crescent flamed into intensely brilliant violet. Then it faded; the whole heaven for a few moments flushed with diffused rose; but the show was over. That supreme flash recalled the pulsing and rutilant coruscations with which Tintoretto spheres his celestial messengers. I could have fancied the crescent and its meteoric emanations to have been the shield of an archangel. On Monte Generoso last spring we watched a sunset of great beauty. Thunder-clouds hung over the extreme heights of Monte Rosa, stationary, like the up-spread wing of a seraph who had plunged headlong down the western steep of flame. All the rest of him was hidden by the mountain: only this one wing, fretted with grain of gold and crimson and deep blue, pointed skyward. And restlessly against the gorgeous glow behind it shot lightning flashes, as though an angelic sword behind the hills were doing dreadfully. Well, the auroral shield was fit buckler for this seraph.

Clifton, now as ever, is full of vague yet powerful associations. When will this Circe cease to brew enchantments for my soul? The trees and streets and distant views of down and valley keep saying to me as I walk, "Put upon your heart the dress which we have woven for you; you will wear it, whether you like or not; palpitate, aspire, recalcitrate as you may, here it is waiting for you!"

VII

I saw a vision of deep eyes
In morning sleep when dreams are true:
Wide humid eyes of hazy blue,
Like seas that kiss the horizon skies.

Then as I gazed, I felt the rain
Of soft warm curls around my cheek,
And heard a whisper low and meek:
"I love, and canst thou love again?"

A gentle youth beside me bent;
His cool moist lips to mine were pressed,
That throbbed and burned with love's unrest:
When, lo, the powers of sleep were spent;

And noiseless on the airy wings
That follow after night's dim way,
The beauteous boy was gone for aye,
A theme of vague imaginings.

Yet I can never rest again:
The flocks of morning dreams are true;
And till I find those eyes of blue
And golden curls, I walk in pain.

VIII

Spring comes again: the blushing earth
Will deck herself with bridal flowers:
The birds among the leafy bowers
Will wake dumb winter's woods with mirth.

But I shall never find him, never:
Though winter's snow dissolve in dew,
And hyacinth's star-spangled blue
'Neath vernal breezes bend and shiver.

The field shall throb with marriage hymn,
And summer's wealth shall deck the grove,
Wherethrough my feet must lonely rove,
Disconsolately seeking him.

Seek on, seek on, till autumn dies
Like sunset in drear winter's night;
Seek on, seek on, for thy delight,
A mirage dream, before thee flies.

Brackets of grey rock jutting from the solid cliff, and shaded by the white leaves of the service-trees. From these perches the eye can plunge into the massy woods beneath. Birches fledging the precipice, feathery ashes, tall limes and glossy oaks mingle the billows of their verdant crests and fill the hollow of the valley. Sometimes a wood-pigeon, pale in sunlight, blue in shadow, passes. The sunlight streams along the ravine, casts purple shade upon the river, strikes in flame against the rich red rocks beyond. The Avon is crowded with ships and boats and steamers. These enliven the waters, ploughing up its solemn shadows and many-hued reflections. Have you noticed that reflections in a stream are more intensely coloured than real objects? The mingling reds and greens upon the river here glow like veined marble. Broken by moving prows into ribs and furrows of shivered opalescence, while the blue sky gleams back from the shadowed sides of wavelets, these many-tinted radii flank the black bulk of sea-going vessels like fins of gorgeous sea-dragons.

Leigh Woods are as beautiful as when I roamed in them three years ago. The lights fall still as golden on those grey rocks streaked with red, on the ivy and the glossy trees, the ferns and heather and enchanter's nightshade. This loveliness sinks into my soul now as it did then. But it does not stir me so profoundly or painfully. I do not feel the unassuaged hunger of the soul so deeply.

IX

The tide is high, and stormy beams
Of sunlight scud across the down:
Above, the cloudy squadrons frown;
On their broad front a rainbow gleams.

Cease, boisterous wind. The west is grey
With glory-coated mists, that swell
From distant seas, and gathering tell
Of coming storm and darkened day.

Leave the dank clouds to droop, and guide
Toward their fair port yon sleeping sails:
Close-furled they wait the wakening gales;
Shower-sprinkled shines the pennon wide.

Sail seaward, stately ship, and view
Some blessèd isle where love is bred.
Bring me again my love that's dead,
And all I have I'll give to you.

The magic of divine spring sunlight is again abroad. The clearings in Leigh Woods are sheets of bluebells. The service-trees upon the cliffs have expanded their white under-leafage, with thick bosses of blossom honey-sweet; burly, big-bodied, furry bees, banded black and red, swaying helplessly, and swinging their unwieldy carcasses in air, hum drunken with honeydew and white bloom above and underneath and all around.

X

*My own loved Clifton, jocund May
Hath decked thy banks and bowers again;
Thy populous elms that crowd the plain,
Thy birches, fountains of green spray.*

*Once more I pace the lonesome woods,
I hear the thrush and cuckoo call,
I hear the tinkling raindrops fall,
I smell the scent of hidden buds.*

*Star-spangled bluebell heavens are spread
'Neath silky screens of tender beech;
The yews their dewy fingers reach
To lay them on the lily bed.*

*All that is fair, and sweet, and gay,
All brightest germs of happy thought,
To-day their freshest gifts have brought
To crown the brows of laughing May.*

*But I am lone, and sad, and dull,
My brain is sick, my heart is dry;
A weary longing dims the sky,
With bitter want my soul is full.*

*Oh, wherefore, wherefore, is he gone?
He made my life one living spring;
My heart was then a joyous thing,
And brightened when the sunbeams shone.*

*I see the light, I see the flowers;
The trees are tremulous with praise;
One craving darkens all my days;
Dead love hath dulled the jocund hours.*

XI

*It seems as though these years of pain
Had never made me man from boy,
So keenly do I feel the joy
That breathes in wakening spring again.*

*The rooks complain of coming showers;
The sharp fresh morning breezes blow;
The sunbeams on the river glow,
And kiss the brows of misty towers;*

*While I along our terrace stray,
I count the shadows on the lawn,
The clouds across the azure drawn
In dappled films of white and grey.*

*All silent signs of spring are rife:
My heart leaps up to hail the hours,
That guerdon bring of vernal flowers,
And swell our veins with love and life.*

*I leap, I cry, "O summer, trace
Thy hues along the deepening wood,
Thy fleecy vapours on the flood,
Thy lush green grasses o'er the chase!*

*"O summer, come! Voluptuous queen,
Bright mistress of a magic wand!
And stir me with thy fairy hand,
And make me what I once have been!*

*"For spring is fresh on mead and hill,
As fresh as those three Aprils gone;
But all my life is dead and wan,
My pulse of love is cold and still.*

> "I count the shadow, count the cloud,
> And hail the growth of silent days;
> But there were other notes of praise,
> With which those springtide hours were loud.
>
> "They sounded in the windy strife,
> I heard them in the dim starlight,
> They shouted through the landscape bright,
> They made me one with nature's life."

We clambered down the cliffs, and bruised young fennel-shoots and marjoram and thyme and the many aromatic mints and celeries that grow there. We saw the thorns in bloom, and the light upon the hanging birches of Leigh Woods, and the jackdaws glistening from shade to sunlight, as of old. Ships came up the Avon at our feet; we could almost touch the pennons waving from their masts. Then we wandered on the downs, whence we could see the channel, silvery-grey like a lake, with film behind film of Welsh hills traced upon the blue beyond. All was so calm, so clear, that the eye might trace elm-masses on the farther marge of Severn, and the hedgerows of the upland fields, with here and there a patch of curling smoke.

XII

> The light from yonder cliff is fled,
> That yester morn so brightly shone;
> The glory of thy love hath gone
> From my dulled life, and left it dead.

Let sunshine fade from rock and sky,
Let Leigh's deep woodland walks be torn;
O'er ruined woods I will not mourn,
Which once were green, when you and I

Went hand in hand among the flowers,
Whose names I taught you, and I made
Rare crowns of columbines to shade
With purple buds the golden showers

Of your loved curls. At times we hung
Like eagles o'er the dizzy rock,
Where faintly boomed the hammer's shock,
And ever upward slowly swung

The sailor's melancholy chant;
While ships went gliding out to sea,
Sails furled and pennons floating free,
With sunlight on their sterns aslant;

Till evening yellowed over all
From Hesper in the dewy sky—
The woods may fall, I will not sigh;
Love's star hath set, 'tis time they fall.

XIII

Three summers gone: and now once more
Pale autumn comes to pluck the leaf;
On every hill they bind the sheaf;
The oak-woods redden as of yore.

The woods may bronze; the golden ears
May gladden all the land with grain;
But I shall never feel again
The gladness of those byegone years.

We climbed down the face of St. Vincent's Rock by a path I know. The full moon was partly hidden by heavy clouds, but the northern sky held delicate green and pale-blue light, and the moon poured oblique rays upon the river and the woods. Then the clouds sailed slowly away, and their edges were tinct with pearl and opal. Spaces of crystalline azure, seas of glass, swam between them, full-filled with moonlight and trembling with scattered stars—stars scarcely seen in that pellucid radiance—stars palpitating, throbbing out breathless melodies. At length the moon emerged, naked and round, glorious, midway above the bridge, suspended in luminous twilight. The cliff shone like marble in her plenilunar splendour. But again the clouds gathered. A vulture's head shot forward and swallowed the moon's silver sphere. Again she triumphed, and this time the clouds dispersed in gauze and filmy veils of faintest shell-like hues. Finally, Queen Luna reigned in undisputed majesty. And now I seemed to see choruses of sylph-like shapes sailing on one side from the valley of Nightingales, and on the other from the shadow of St. Vincent's Rock, to meet and weave their dances in the air; and now an arm was thrust from the Giant's Cave, which grew and grew until the huge hand rested on my heart; and now furry paws of monsters from beneath were laid upon the knoll beside me; and now I saw the blanched face of Lilith upturned imploring from the smooth slope of the curving rock above; and then again came troops of shadows sweeping down the path which we had traversed; and yet again the gleaming scales of dragons coiled and twisted on the glittering mud-banks of Avon, and all their massive jaws were raised to hiss.

After midnight I came home through the avenue of Clifton churchyard, and emerged upon the open space beyond. The valley of the Avon was flooded with moonlight; fleeces of almost iridescent cloud hung to westward, and the sulphurous glare of Ashton furnaces sent out flame and smoke into that liquid argent of moon-bathed wood and hill and meadow.

XIV

How coldly steals the journeying night,
How silent sleeps the garden spray:
Far down I hear the watch-dog bay;
I hear the sheep from yonder height.

Swathed in thick mist the city lies:
Her lamps like myriad jewels peer
Through wreaths of vapour faintly clear;
Her chimes from muffled belfries rise.

Pale as the moon is memory's light,
Those April days as darkly lower,
As looms mid yonder mist the tower,
Which then with rays of morn were bright.

I hear his voice like yon thin chimes;
As those faint lamps his eyes are dim,
Deep midnight gloom encircles him,
Scarce can I dream of those dear times.

It is five o'clock in the morning. The sun has not yet touched the horizon, but the sky is yellow, barred with rose, and the morning star is shining in pale blue above. The city lies wrapped in thick white vapour; only the towers of Redclyffe and the Cathedral rising like black islands. Here and there trees and grassy knolls emerge from the level sea of mist. Our garden and the distant hills are clear in garish light of morning. The whole scene is very silent and asleep, chill with dews, the foliage stiff with frosty lack of warmth, the birds half waking. Thus, as with life itself, only the great things remain distinct to catch fading or growing lights of sunset or of sunrise, while all around is blurred and indistinct. Last evening the red blaze of the west fell upon those towers with such splendour as memory throws upon the past. This morning they stand forth like ominous events to be—sorrow and death, thick-shadowed, seen only by their certainty of darkness. The past glows with a sunset flush of poetry. The future is cold with sad features sharply defined. But the past fades into indistinctness, while the future broadens into perfect clarity of day.

XV

To thee far off, more far than death,
To thee I make my lonely rhyme,
Condemned to see thee not in time,
Though life and love still rule thy breath.

Our pulses beat, our hearts strike on;
They beat, but do not beat together;
Our years are young, but lusty weather
Wakes in our blood no unison.

We pace the self-same field and street,
We hear the same strong organ roll;
No music leaps from soul to soul,
Our paths are near, yet never meet.

Only in visions of the night
I seem with thee to watch the morn;
A tempest swells, and thou art borne
To lands I know not far from sight.

NOTES OF A SOMERSETSHIRE HOME

(*SUTTON COURT*)

I

" PER noctis vigilias clamavi, et lacrymis torum meum irrigavi. Mane lucem spectare odi, e sub vespere tenebras perhorreo. Ab urbe in rus, solatium dolorisque lenimenta desiderans, effugi. Mecum autem me portabam, nec mei met ipsius desidiem deponere potui. Quod non est, quæro ; quod est, fastidior ; præterita respicio, nec tamen lætabundus sum ; præsentia me cruciant ; futura timeo. Amare nequeo quos amare debuissem. Amore inamabili eorum quos amare nunquam potuerim, ardeo. Erroris atque imbecillitatis meæ mihi conscius, non tamen me talibus e volutabris evehere jam valeo. Lux me tædet, nox me terret, libri fatigant, homines contemnunt. Nihil invenio quod vulnus medeat, nihil quod sinu meo foveam, nihil quod osculer, nihil quod precibus et votis colam. Erro miserabilis ; inter vivos mortuus ; inter frutices alga ; inter stellas caligo ; inter dulciloquas volucres silentium ; inter amantes invidia ; inter sapientes stultus ; inter felices infelix ; inter divites pauperrimus. Sine spe, sine luce, sine viribus, sine animo, cur terram onero ?"

In the afternoon I said, "This melancholy is nigh to madness." And in truth, what with unhealthy sleep by night and painful reflection by day, I seem to be losing the power of living as reason and will direct. Yet in the clear September sky, as I walked to Dundry and back, misery fell from me like a burden. I gathered from the hedgerow a long tendril of convolvulus bronzed by sunlight and polished by the kisses of the summer air. And this I twined about my hat. Strange heart of man! How we yearn with fever after knowledge, and then sicken of disgust for thought and speculation! How we sink numbed into week-long monotony, although Nature surrounds us with beauty and love, and then by some fine touch upon our senses wake to sympathy with Fauns!

Sept. 1862.

II

We spend our days lazily and quietly, and have as much sunshine as is common in the

West. Though it rains one day, the next brings splendid clouds—domes and columns of white alabaster moulded into the most stately forms, and sailing slowly over the blue sky with bars and tatters of grey vapour on their fronts. To-day we sat in Broad Mead, looking up at them and watching a herd of cattle. Twenty-nine were browsing in front of us, with heads bent down and tails lazily switching off the flies. One heard them feeding as they cropped the grass and champed it in their mouths. I thought of Wordsworth's line:

There are forty feeding like one.

We had rambled through the lanes and fields to Stanton Drew, over the clover, by hedgerows tangled thick with briony—black, yellow, and green-berried. When we reached "the stones," as they call them here, we sat down in the inner circle of the Druid's temple. It was a pleasant scene—the masses of red crystalline rock, overgrown with moss and lichen, standing in a ring about the centre of the field. Other remains of broken circles lie about the meadow, some thrown down and some erect, some perfect and some shattered, but all picturesquely purple and gigantic. Pigmy English cows were grazing near us, and a little rustic stream, belted with alders and aspens, ran silently at one end of the field. Behind us rose the church-tower and a manor-house, and above all the marble pinnacles and bubbles of the clouds. C. said the whole scene seemed to say "Summer." On a distant hill stretched cornfields, yellow, and ready for the harvest, with green hedges running round and through their cloth of gold. The sounds of country-folk speaking to their cattle and of dogs from the farm-yards came to us in the stillness.

Yesterday we took another walk of the same kind. Edward drove us to Chew-Magna, and from there we walked to Dundry. We found ferns in the quarries, and looked down on Bristol, a fairy city in the valley of the Avon. It is pleasant walking here with C. We both of us love to search for wild flowers, and from some high hill to gaze on "distant colour, happy hamlet"—the blue Mendips with their robe of wood and few faint towers and villages. In the narrow lanes we stop to examine what she calls "Nature's vulgar embroidery"—ferns, violet leaves, great bunches of the red Guelder-rose-berries, enchanter's nightshade, white bindweed, marsh-mallow, and cascades of clematis. I remember wandering here alone three autumns ago. How I bowed myself in anguish on Dundry hill, and walking home crowned myself with black briony leaves, and forgot my wish to die.

In the night I dreamed that I met Willie at the door of the Cathedral—as he used to be, and as I used to be—but years had passed away, and we had not seen each other. He said with his eyes, " Friend, have you come at last ? I have waited for you as a watcher waiteth for the morning "—his old words. He took me by the hand, and we sat together in an aisle and heard windy chaunts sweep through the darkness as in days gone by. I woke up well, and it was morning.

To-day we have been at Cheddar. It was quite dull and cloudy when we left, but the sun came out on Mendip, and shone brightly all the rest of the day. The rocks at Cheddar deserve their fame for picturesqueness. The gorge is so narrow and so well proportioned that the 480 feet of cliff might stand for as many thousands. The windings of the road continually open out fresh beauties, and aid to create an illusion of vastness. In some places the columns, spires, and bastions of rock impend and topple with an oppressive menace on the road. What Cheddar wants is water. It is absolutely voiceless. With a few cascades and a torrent running beneath the road, it might resemble an Alpine pass. I thought of Wordsworth's lines on Gondo. " The unfettered clouds and region of the heavens," the "winds thwarting winds bewildered and forlorn," were there; but no "black drizzling crags that spake by the wayside as if a voice were in them," no "stationary blasts of waterfalls," no "sick sight and giddy prospect of the raving stream." With eyes accustomed to the Alps, one was always longing for a foot or so of unmistakable snow-summit above the limestone, to make one feel that the crowning patches of bright grass were the beginning of pastures leading up to glacier and tracts of ice. Yet this ravine is in no sense Swiss. It is more like the Saxon Switzerland, still more like some road across the Apennines—that gorge beyond Urbino on the way to Gubbio, for instance —but really *sui generis*. This is its charm. The veins of ivy clinging to the highest spires, the fern-fledged basements, the rock-pluming yew trees, and the silence of the calm grey cliffs, belong to Somersetshire. I climbed one side of the valley, and saw Sedgmoor beyond, with Glastonbury Tor and the broad champaign stretching to the Severn. C. and I went down into a cave. The drapery of stalactite is very beautiful. It hangs in transparent masses like the folds of an Ionic chiton. The lights, too, in the cavern are so variously disposed about its strange recesses, that one seems to be looking at the work of fairy masons and sculptors, lit by fairy lamps.

This afternoon C. has been sketching and I watching her. We sat in the field opposite the house, just where the ground falls away to the gully. In old times the stream made a lake here, and hollowed out a great bed for itself with shelving sides. Now it has retreated, leaving a green sward that slopes by gentle undulations to the gully. Trees have grown up round the water, oaks above with gnarled arms lichen-grey, alders beneath, and elfin ashes rising like spirits with frail stems and pallid tresses from the deeper green. Over the grass a light of laughing flowers is spread—not violets now, but crocuses, lilac and white, which do not fear the sun, but spread their faces broadly to his rays. How they glow! red in the sunlight and pale purple in the shadows, each a perfect form. Lady's tresses, like fairy wands, hung with pearly bells, odorous and dewy, stand among blue milkwort blossoms, and on every hawkweed rests an azure butterfly. There are multitudes here. The rooks, ever so far away, high up in the sky, caw faintly. The air is loud with humming flies. Pink cloudlets scarcely move across the blue, which is no darker than the white part of a beauty's eye. The whole field undulates and ripples like a sea in ages far ago, before Atlantics and Pacifics were divided, and when the ocean waves went round the world. Each billow is gigantic, and the grass shines like an Alpine pasture in the sun. Elm shadows fall athwart these undulations, and the restless fretwork of ash branches, with ponderous darkness from the brooding oaks.

All this I saw. But to me now a primrose is a primrose and a field a field. " For this, for everything, I am out of tune." Why so, faint heart? A sore brain, bad thoughts, and discontent. I would not so much mind if I could do my work. But even there I fail. I toiled at Marston's comedies to-day, and wrote such antiquated nonsense. *Crambe repetita* is nothing to my salad, which consists of the very refuse of a kitchen-garden gathered from a dustheap and served up with ashes.

I know that this land is passing fair; but I am not a part of it. The hushed stillness of the hanging woods, the dells in which Pan cools himself in noontide heat among rank ferns and dripping mosses, the pendulous abeles, the free spring of tall aspiring limes affording pasture to a million bees, the indescribable low sounds which Nature makes alone unto herself, half melodies, music without a thought, all preluding to man; the quick rush of water over stones by reeds and cresses in the brook, the crowns of briony which Dryads weave, the clematis which braids thick-berried banks, the gossamers where fairies swing and whistle to the bats their steeds, glowworms hanging out faint lamps to lure ethereal suitors, like Moore's ladies whom the angels loved, white mists at morning and cold dews at night, the multitudinous stars, unchanging galaxies and glimmering constellations, the low voice of birds before the sun slants upward from the underworld, the magnificent swoop and twitter of the swallow, faint crescents of young moons in liquid skies—I used to know and love them all.

August 1869.

III

We are just at the end of a fortnight's visit at Sutton Court. The weather has not favoured us. We have only had one really fine day. During the rest of the time one long succession of westerly gales has brought wind and rain in hurricanes across the sky, and we have stayed indoors, escaping to the fields by runs and sallies in the intervals of sunshine. Yet this very intermittency of fine weather is most beautiful. If I were inclined to write a study of Somersetshire, the place would supply me with plenty of motives and of pretty pictures. It is a true realisation of the ideal primitive English Country, where railways have not yet penetrated, where the corn-land is still allowed to have its fallow year, and the hedges stretch unpruned across the fields in spite of modern farming. These fields are, each in itself, a perfect picture—in spring-time yellow with cowslips, in autumn purple with crocuses; and the hedges line them with sweet violets, and primroses, and hyacinths in April, yielding to summer flowers—bindweed, and clematis, and mallow, and wild roses, and St. John's wort—until August brings the scarlet briony berries, and arum bunches of red fruit, and fluffy thistles, and ripe hazels and blackberries. In and out among the bushes grow tangles of enchanter's nightshade, and brake, and hart's tongue, and herb-robert, and broad-feathery ferns. They are a kingdom for the children, lining the green pastures and the deeply cloven lanes—lanes which once were watercourses, and still wind between the slopes of rising hills. Alders and oaks wave over them, and in their cool depth all things are turned "to a green thought in a green shade." The earth in them is mostly of a dark red, and the cottage walls, which are hidden at the turns and angles of the bosky dells, by little rivulets and copses of hazel, show white fronts, jessamine and rose-embowered, against dark boughs. One farm, which is called "Moorledge," seems quite lost and forgotten in a maze of winding leafy lanes and undulating fields, interpreting its own name by the near proximity of rush-grown common land, where the geese run cackling on a windy day. Then there are the "gullies," so called in Somersetshire; other counties call them "bourns," or "chines," or "goyles," or "ghylls;" the bowery courses of little streams, cut in the bosom of the open fields, and grown with every kind of tree—alder, wych-elm, hazel, and oak, and slender ash. By their brinks the briar and burdock, the hemlock and wild rose, the service tree and maple cluster in a leafy jungle, odorous with aromatic herbs, and bright with butterflies, and loud with humming bees. Kingfishers and waterfowl haunt the reeds that grow beneath; and where the water spreads itself into pools, there spring tall bulrushes and beautiful pink willow-herbs and purple loosestrife. To the edge of these ponds come the cattle; for every field is full of grazing kine—the wealth and pride of the country. You see them feeding by scores, gathering at noontide under the spreading boughs of oak or beech in the centre of the meadow, or lowing in the evening on their way to being milked. Nor is the country all so purely pastoral. There is Dundry with its high-towered church, sacred to St. Michael, commanding that view across Bristol and the valley of the Avon, over to Severn and the hills of Wales—a bleak beacon-height, never quiet from the turbulent wind. There is Mendip, 1000 feet above the sea, wooded at its base and springing to open moorland, a bare upland swept by the winter gales, where trees are bent to eastward, puny thorns and a few stubborn oaks, and where the barren fields are separated from each other by stone walls. The ridge of Mendip is always hazy with Atlantic mists and watery west-winds; great clouds seem always forming on its brow, with hazy outlines and brief interspace of bright blue sky—true sea-clouds, gathered far away, and blown by restless south-west gales across the fertile plains. This is why Somersetshire is so rich a pasture-land.

The moisture never fails, and the sun is warm enough to make it foster every kind of herb, and grass, and tree. Autumn is the time for apple-harvest, when you see in every orchard boys and girls shaking the red and golden fruit down to the rank grass below. Baskets, and rakes, and ladders lie about beneath the trees, and a sound of laughing, and of rustling boughs, and of apples pattering like a hailstorm, rings through the home-garth. Then you find a heap of ruddy pippins and brown russettings laid in the darkness of a barn, with mellow October sunlight falling on them through the chinks, while the cider-press is turned outside, and the thick pulpy juice comes foaming into vats and jars. Autumn is the time for apple-harvest, summer for haymaking. There is little corn to cut or ground to till; for pasture is the wealth and beauty of the land. The village must not be forgotten—Stowey, with its thatches and bright gardens, its noble beeches and elms about the little church, its cottage doors embowered in deadly nightshade to protect the house from witchcraft. Nor yet the Court —stately avenues, and terraces, and gardens— homelike, and primitive, and unassuming, where everything is so green that you cannot say where garden ends and fields begin, what is natural and what is the result of art. To the north stretches an ancient avenue of elms, the haunt of rooks— to the south an avenue of limes, the summer home of innumerable bees, and wood-pigeons, and night-flying owls. The Court itself has a long and curious pedigree. Leland says that in the reign of Edward III. one John de Sutton held half a knight's fee, and to him belonged in all probability the tower which forms the oldest and most central building of the Court. It has three storeys; the lowest was where they penned the cattle; the second formed the living and the eating place for masters and men; in the third they slept; and on the roof was the watch-tower, beacon bracket, and crenellations for defence. To this tower in times of greater security was added a large hall, square, roomy, with an ample porch and deep bay windows, and minstrels' gallery above the dais, and yawning chimney : beyond the hall in process of time was placed on one side the kitchen, on the other side the solar room or sunny parlour. The old archways of the hall have Gothic mouldings, showing them to have preceded Tudor times. Before these alterations were effected, the St. Loes, a knightly family of the West, now quite extinct, had become possessors of the Court. Their arms are carved on the stonework of the kitchen window. From the St. Loes it passed in the reign of Elizabeth to the Countess of Salisbury, building Bess of Hardwick, who married a St. Loe for her last husband. She added a chapel to the Court, and made other substantial alterations which have subsisted till this day. After her it came into the possession of the Stracheys. During all its changes the Court has never entirely lost the embattled wall which ran round the house, enclosing a good portion of ground. To the south, and east, and west it has been destroyed ; but to the north it still stands, overgrown with lichens and bushes flowering from its cracks —a remnant of the ancient state of warfare and defence. Pear trees, and figs, and hollyhocks, entangled with creeping nasturtiums, and sweet peas, and clematis, make its southern aspect gay and green, while, over all, the frowning battlements stand grey and gloomy like the wrecks of a past state of things. Nor is the house without its ghosts. There is a tradition that the wall was built by Giant St. Loe, as he is called among the rustics. While he was building it, there came a neighbouring giant, who jeered at him and said: " Is this your wall of protection? Lo! I will leap over it." This he did, like Remus; but Giant St. Loe went on building, and never cared for him at all. Well, this giant who built the wall, still haunts the Court, and up and down the turret staircase on winter nights goes clanking with his iron heel and jingling spurs. A sadder story is the tale of a young daughter of the house who drowned herself for love in the gully at the end of the lime avenue, and who still is seen, a white form, sheeted and shrill-screaming, in the Black Walk underneath the chestnut trees. Round the old hall hang the portraits of many generations—Elizabethan ruffs, Puritan Geneva collars, Sir Peter Lely ladies with lambs, a whole family attired like Roman warriors of the age of Anne, Romneys and Beecheys and Northcotes of a recent date. Every degree of stiffness, primness, smirk, melancholy, vacancy, intensity, gravity, levity, stern manliness, and maiden prettiness—warriors, and citizens, and shepherdesses, and admirals, and lords—look down upon us as we dine.

August 1866.

IV

Spring has come suddenly, with cuckoos, blackbirds, and thrushes. The chestnuts are bursting into leaf and cones of snowy blossom; laburnums and lilacs in flower; with a wonderful wealth of cowslip, bluebell, speedwell, allium, red lychnis, orchis, dog-violet, and starwort in fields and hedges. Primroses, too, linger, though faint; and the wood anemones are still like tears or dew among deep grasses. Thus spring and summer kiss each other. The trees of every kind display their earliest, tenderest foliage, scarce-fledged. Orchards everywhere are snowy-pink; and overhead there is the purest sky, with soft winds from the Channel. We strolled down to the stream, where C. showed me a little dell brimful of thick blue hyacinths. Then we went through meadows, picking cowslips and orchises, watching the distance over Mendip and Chew-Magna—a picture of most perfect spring and hallowing tranquillity.

The hyacinths in these deep sunken lanes, mingling with cowslips and cuckoo-flowers, present the very bloom and beauty of the year. Yet they are less lovely in the hedges than when they blend with the same cuckoo-flowers and cowslips on the slopes of short green grass, with blue distance in front and the golden foliage of thorn and oak above. Such slopes rival any Alpine meadow. This early spring is like the first dawn of love, before fruition, when all is still conjecture and anticipation, when a hand-touch is more passionate than the nights of satisfied desire that are to follow. Of all spring flowers, the hyacinths attract me most. Their beauty is pathetic: tall stem and melancholy curve and fringed bells amethystine, the divine burden of youthful curls. As they line the lanes in twilight, a mist of blueness, they seem to murmur music.

April 1870.

CULTURE: ITS MEANING AND ITS USES

NOT many years ago, I happened to notice the review of one of my books in some weekly periodical. The writer sneered at me for travelling round Europe with a portmanteau full of culture on my back. This made me reflect. What does the reviewer mean by culture? What is it I am supposed to stagger under like a pedlar's pack? And then, what do *I* mean by culture? How do *I* value the wares I carry on my shoulders? Reflection convinced me that the reviewer and myself held different opinions about what we both call culture.

It is probable that when people use this word, nowadays, it signifies for them some knowledge of history and literature, intelligence refined by considerable reading, and a susceptibility to the beauties of art and nature. But words which have been overworked, or which have passed into the jargon of cliques, are apt to acquire a secondary and degraded meaning with the general public. And this has been the case with culture. All the good things it implies in common parlance are understood to be alloyed with pedantry, affectation, æsthetical priggishness. It is believed that the cultured person, like the dilettante of a previous century, will rave about the Correggiosity of Correggio, the symbolic depth of Botticelli, the preciousness of Ruskin's insight into Tintoretto. Or, if he does not take that line, he may be expected to possess a multifarious store of knowledge about all periods of all the arts and literatures, and to be perpetually parading this knowledge in and out of season.

The last sort of stuff is, probably, what my reviewer accused me of hawking over Europe. But this, I am certain, is not what I mean when I talk of culture.

Judged by the etymology of the word, culture is not a natural gift. It implies tillage of the soil, artificial improvement of qualities supplied by nature. It is clearly, then, something acquired, as the lovelinesses of the garden rose are developed from the briar, or the "savage-tasted drupe" becomes "the suave plum" by cultivation. In the full width of its meaning, when applied to human beings, culture is the raising of faculties—physical, mental, emotional, and moral—to their highest excellence by training. In a particular sense, and in order to distinguish culture from education, it implies that this training has been consciously carried on by the individual. Education educes or draws forth faculties. Culture improves, refines, and enlarges them, when they have been brought out. Finally, although moral and physical qualities are susceptible of both education and culture, yet it is commonly understood, when we use these terms, that we are thinking of the intellectual faculties. This is specially the case with culture. It would be pedantry to extend its sphere to morals and athletics; we cannot talk of a cultured gymnast or a cultured philanthropist, for instance, when we are referring to a man who has trained either his muscles or his benevolent emotions to their highest excellence.

I will therefore define culture, for the purpose of this discussion, as the raising of previously educated intellectual faculties to their highest potency by the conscious effort of their possessors.

In its most generalised significance, culture may be identified with self-effectuation. The individual attempts to arrive at his real self, to perfect the rudiments supplied by Nature on the line for which he is best qualified, and by so doing to arrive at independence—what the Germans call *Selbstständigkeit*. Men of true culture, as distinguished from that false thing which usurps the name, may possess diverse intellectual temperaments, and reach widely-separated points of vantage. But they agree in this, that each has acquired freedom from bondage to cliques and schools, from the prejudices of the worser and the fashions of the better vulgar. Goethe points out in two famous lines that this self-effectuation, which is the highest end of culture, demands different environments according to the different quality of the mental force to be developed:

> *Es bildet ein Talent sich in der Stille,*
> *Sich ein Charakter in dem Strom der Welt.*

"Talent forms itself in the silence of the study, character in the stream of the great world." But when formed, each mental force, whether it belongs to the contemplative or to the active order, each self, so cultivated, will possess the privilege insisted on by the same poet of being able "to live resolvedly in the Whole, the Good, the Beautiful": not in the warped, the falsified, the egotistical; not in the petty, the adulterated, the partial; not in the school, the clique, the coterie; but in the large sphere of universal and enduring ideas.

It will be seen now that, when I speak of

culture. I mean something different from what is commonly intended by the half-slang phrase. It may be urged I am ascribing too lofty and indefinite a function to culture, when I define it to be the raising of intellectual faculties to their highest potency by means of conscious training. Still, the more we think about the derivation and the history of the word, the more shall we become convinced that this is its root meaning, its most abstract and essential signification. It is the duty of criticism always to aim at bringing back abused or debased words, so far as this is possible, to their logical and legitimate values.

But now comes the question, How is the man with educated faculties to achieve culture ? In the case of rare and specially gifted natures, there is no need to ask this question. They attain culture, and more than it can give, by an act of instinct. They leap to their work impulsively, discover it inevitably. Owen Meredith, the late Lord Lytton, wrote no stronger line than this, which I quote from memory :

Genius does what it must, but talent does what it can.

In trying to solve the problem of culture, we are bound to leave genius unreckoned. The force implied in what we call genius is incalculable, uncontrollable. Genial natures are often doomed to frosts and thwartings; are sometimes favoured by the grace of circumstance; are never fostered by prescribed rules and calculated issues. Handel, with nothing but a purely professional education, soared far higher into the ideal regions of his art than Mendelssohn with all the culture Germany could give him. Shakespeare, a mere playwright and theatre-lessee, darted his rays of dramatic insight far deeper and far wider than Goethe, who was nursed upon the lore and wisdom of all ages. Genius is the pioneer whom talent follows; and men of culture have been mostly talents, though we can discover here and there a genius among their ranks. In dealing with culture, then, we have to regard the needs of talent rather than the necessities of genius: intellectual faculties of good quality, rather than minds of an exceptional, unique distinction.

Culture is self-tillage, the ploughing and the harrowing of self by use of what the ages have transmitted to us from the work of gifted minds. It is the appropriation of the heritage bequeathed from previous generations to the needs and cravings of the individual in his emancipation from "that which binds us all, the common." It is the method of self-exercise which enables a man, by entering into communion with the greatest intellects of past and present generations, by assimilating the leading ideas of the World-

Spirit, to make himself, according to his personal capacity, an efficient worker, if not a creator, in the symphony for ever woven out of human souls.

There are two principal methods for arriving at the ends involved in culture. These may be briefly described as Humanism and Science. In a certain sense, we owe both to that mighty intellectual movement of the fifteenth and sixteenth centuries with which the term Renaissance is commonly connected. The so-called Reformation movement was a subordinate, though politically important, stream of its main current. The essential element in this great burst of energy has been well defined in Michelet's famous formula: the re-discovery of the world and of man. It began with the revival of learning, or the return of the mediæval mind to fountain-heads of knowledge and of life-experience gushing from long-neglected antique sources. At first, as was natural, the study of mankind in ancient languages and literatures and histories, in Hebrew, Greek, and Roman records, arrested curiosity. Humanism—the literary, philosophical, historical, artistic side of culture—gave tone to European thought for many generations. Still, it was impossible to pursue these studies of the past without raising comparison with the present. The remoteness of the modern from the antique mind led to critical analysis ; and out of criticism emerged science. Science includes all branches of exact co-ordinated knowledge. Criticism, exerted first upon texts and theories, began to be extended to facts. In course of time the study of Nature evolved itself out of the study of ancient philosophies. The curiosity about the external world, which had at first been poetical, æsthetic, sensuous, assumed the gravity of anxious speculation and of careful inquiry into actual conditions of existence. Mathematics, in the field of physics and astronomy, introduced novel conceptions of the universe. Without tracing the evolution of the natural sciences, it is enough to observe that at the end of the last century Europe became aware that humanism alone would not suffice as the basis of education and culture. The Renaissance had rediscovered man and the world. The criticism of man implied humanism. The criticism of the world, at a somewhat later period, led to science. Science, though tardy to emerge, proved itself the paramount force of the modern as distinguished from the antique and the mediæval spirit. The whole of this nineteenth century has been dominated by a rapid extension of scientific ideas. Scientific methods have been introduced into every department of study. We have arrived at the conviction that mental training of a thorough sort cannot neglect science. In other words, we know now that an interpenetration of humanism with science and of science with humanism is the condition of the highest culture. At present the fusion cannot be said to have been fully realised. And for the future it is probable that there will always be two differently constituted orders of minds, the one inclining to the purely humanistic, and the other to the purely scientific side of culture.

I have no wish to enter here into the controversy which has been carried on between scientific men and humanists as to the relative educational value of their methods. Nor do I want to touch upon the burning question as to whether the classics will have to be abandoned in our schools. I shall content myself by pointing out that if, as Pope says, "the proper study of mankind is man," then humanism must always keep the first rank in the higher intellectual culture. It cannot be dethroned by abstract mathematics. or by the investigation of the physical universe. Ideal culture involves both factors; and this ideal was to some extent realised in Goethe. Few men—none, indeed—can hope now to exercise themselves completely in both branches. We have to choose between the alternatives of a literary or a scientific training. Still, the points of contact between humanism and science are so numerous that thorough study compels us to approach literature scientifically and also to pursue science in a humane spirit. The humanist remembers that his department is capable of being treated with something like the exactitude which physical research demands. The man of science bears in mind that he cannot afford to despise imagination and philosophy. Both poetry and metaphysic, upon the one hand, contributed to the formation of the evolutionary hypothesis. Without habits of strict investigation, on the other hand, we should not possess the great historical works of the nineteenth century, its discoveries in comparative philology, its ethnological theories and inquiries into primitive conditions of society.

I have been speaking about culture as a form of self-effectuation through conscious training of the mind. It is a psychical state, so to speak, which may be acquired by sympathetic and assimilative study. It makes a man to be something; it does not teach him to create anything. It has no power to stand in the place of Nature, and to endow a human being with new faculties. It prepares him to exert his innate faculties in a chosen line of work, with a certain spirit of freedom, with a certain breadth of understanding.

This brings me to consider the relation of culture to those special industries, arts, and professions which are determined by the subdivision of labour and by the varieties of human temperament. We have seen already that "genius does what it must." Education and self-training exercise but slender formative influence over natures like Michael Angelo, Beethoven, Shakespeare. This is the pith of the old proverb that "a poet is born, not made." Some of the greatest men of genius, Burns and Turner for example, can hardly be called men of culture. Others, like Ben Jonson, Tasso, Heine, were so emphatically. We have also seen that "Talent does what it can." For this reason, culture is most important to men of talent. It enables them to know what they can do; brings forth their latent capacities; leads them to choose painting or sculpture, pure literature or philosophy, according to their innate bias. It also compensates that bias by giving them a general sympathy with things outside their speciality. In this respect it is of value also for men of genius, whose bias in one particular direction reaches the maximum. Specialists, unless they be creative geniuses of the most marked type, require to be armed by culture against narrow-mindedness and the conceit of thinking that their own concerns are all-important. A man of moderate ability who cannot see beyond the world of beetles, beyond the painter's studio, beyond the church or chapel, beyond the concert room, beyond the grammar of an extinct language, or some one period of history, is apt to be intolerable. Culture teaches him his modest place in the whole scheme. Culture is, therefore, absolutely essential to the mental well-being of persons confined by their craft or profession to a narrow range of intellectual interests. I am, of course, not alluding here to handicraftsmen and honest labourers, who do the work required of them without self-conceit, and serve the immediate needs of society without being aware of their own inestimable value. But, to return to the intellectual specialist. It is fortunate for him that the downright examination of any branch of knowledge, the conscientious practice of any fine art, directs a man of ordinary talent on the path of real culture. This is due to the inter-connection of all departments in the scheme of modern thought. Humanists and scientists have been engaged together for nearly five centuries in weaving a magic robe, warp and woof combined into one fabric, which gradually through their accumulated industry, approximates to something like an organic tissue. The hope of the future is that any exact investigation of one part will imply an adequate acquaintance with the whole. An able man, therefore, who has made himself an accomplished specialist, will even now be found to have in him the spirit of true culture. That is to say, he will regard his own subject as one province of a vast, pehaps an illimitable, empire.

In a certain sense all people who have developed their own nature to the utmost are specialists. We give the name, indeed, to botanists and oculists, palæographers and lepidopterists, because these men devote their faculties to very strongly demarcated fields of study. But, if we regard the problem from the point of view of personality, the specialist is one who applies the whole of his energies to the single task for which he is specifically qualified. I mean it is no less a speciality in philosophers like Hegel, Comte, and Herbert Spencer, to attempt the co-ordination of all human knowledge in one system, than it is a speciality in men like Ehrenberg and Edison to concentrate their attention upon infusoria and electricity. Both types of individuals, those who strive to embrace the whole, and those who delve into a portion, stand in the same need of culture. I am speaking of culture now under its moral aspect, as teaching us to measure any man's littleness against the vastness of the whole. Auguste Comte, to take an example of one sort, was deficient in the spirit of real culture, because he thought he could reconstitute religion on a fanciful basis.

Darwin was not deficient in this spirit of real culture, because he published his epoch-making theory as a simple hypothesis, restraining himself to rigorous inductions and to limited deductions within a certain sphere of knowledge. No one was more aware than Darwin that he had made a serious contribution to his own branch of science. But no one was more conscious of the immense dark sphere of inscrutabilities surrounding the little spark of light he had evoked.

I must repeat that culture is not an end in itself. It prepares a man for life, for work, for action, for the reception and emission of ideas. Life itself is larger than literature, than art, than science. Life does not exist for them, but they for life. This does not imply that it is better to be a man of no culture than a man of culture. The man of culture is obviously capable of living to more purpose, of getting a larger amount out of life, than the man of no culture. He can also judge more fairly in all cases of comparative criticism. Still, I am unable to perceive that the refinements of the intellect on any line of its development involve an ennobling or a strengthening of the human being. Given individuals of equal calibre, as many wise men may be found among the artisans and peasants as among reputed *savants*. Household proverbs are not unfrequently a safer guide to conduct than the aphorisms of professors. We all of us probably have known flawless characters, men, as the Greeks said, "four-cornered without defect," who never enjoyed the privileges of education. The life of no great nation lies either in humanism or science. The arts and literature of Italy in the sixteenth century did not make her powerful or virtuous. The so-called progress to which she is now sacrificing the monuments of her past, a progress dominated by scientific notions, has substituted ugliness and vulgarity for beauty and distinction, without adding an iota to her strength or general intelligence. We ought not to despise culture. The object of this article is to demonstrate its value. But the nearer a man has come to possessing it, the less will he over-estimate acquirements or accumulations of knowledge, the more importance will he attach to character, to personality, to energy, to independence.

At this point it may be useful to glance at the polemic which Walt Whitman, the prophet-poet of democracy, used to carry on against culture. His arguments, to a large extent, miss their mark, because they are directed against the vulgar conception of culture, as an imitative smattering, a self-assertiveness of so-called cultivated people. He has ignored the higher significance which may be given to the word, and which I have sought to bring forth. Yet much that he said is worthy of attention. He endeavoured to enforce the truth that a great and puissant nation does not live by sensibility and knowledge, but by the formation of character, by the development of personal energy. "What is our boasted culture?" he asks. "Do you term that perpetual, pistareen, paste-pot work American art, American drama, taste, &c.?" Culture is good in its way; but it is not what forms a manly personality, a sound and simple faith. "As now taught, accepted, and carried out, are not the processes of culture rapidly creating a class of supercilious infidels, who believe in nothing?" "Shall a man lose himself in countless masses of adjustments, and be so shaped with reference to this, that, and the other that the simply good and healthy and brave parts of him are reduced and chipped away, like the bordering of box in a garden?" The only culture which is of service to a nation must aim less at polish than at the bracing of character. "It must have for its spinal meaning the formation of typical personality of character, eligible to the uses of the high average of men, and not restricted by conditions ineligible to the masses." To the man of letters he exclaims :—

What is this you bring?
Is it not something that has been better told or done before?

> *Have you not imported this, or the spirit of it,*
>   *in some ship?*
> *Is it not a mere tale? a rhyme? a prettiness?*

And again:

> *Rhymes and rhymers pass away, poems distilled*
>   *from poems pass away;*
> *The swarms of reflectors and the polite pass, and*
>   *leave ashes;*
> *Admirers, importers, obedient persons, make but*
>   *the soil of literature.*

The pith of his contention lies in the following admonition, which breathes the spirit of an antique Spartan or Roman: " Fear grace, elegance, civilisation, delicatesse." Shun the atmosphere which enfeebles, the learning which encumbers, the customs and traditions which trammel independence. Prophetic utterances of this sort are apt to be exaggerated. It is good, however, that cultured people should be told not to let culture draft them into cliques and coteries, separate them from the people, blunt them to the main thought-currents and vital interests of their age.

No great and spontaneous growths of art have arisen in an age of erudition and assimilation. The Greek drama, the Gothic style of architecture, the romantic drama of Elizabethan England, were products not of cultivated taste, but of instinctive genius. There is profound truth in what Herder taught to the young Goethe, that really great poetry has always been the product of a national spirit, and not the product of studies confined to a select few.

No one feels this more than one who, like myself, has devoted a large portion of his life to the history of that period which developed modern culture. I mean the Italian Renaissance. Humanism inflicted an irreparable damage on the national literature of Italy. It impeded the evolution of the mother-tongue by the preference given to composition in dead languages. It caused an abrupt division between the learned classes and the people. When men of genius began again to use Italian for great works of art, they found themselves hampered in two ways. They were clogged with classical reminiscences and precedents. They were separated from popular sympathy and deprived of popular support. The masterpieces of their predecessors, Petrarch and Boccacio, had become classics, and were slavishly imitated. It was not in the lyric or the drama, but in the plastic arts, that the national genius of the Italians expressed itself during the fifteenth and sixteenth centuries.

Germany presents a parallel instance. It is in music that the modern Germans have displayed their national originality. Yet the Germans have been the most thoroughly cultivated of the European nations during the last century and a half. That is to say, they have worked at both branches of culture, humanism and science, with the greatest diligence, and have applied both to literary studies with the most philosophical breadth of intelligence. It cannot be said, however, that the creative literature of this cultured race, in poetry, oratory, the drama, and the novel, taken as a whole, has been of the highest order. It is true that their representative man of genius, the Olympian Goethe, was essentially a poet of culture; and he shows to what altitudes the cultivated intellect may climb, when it resides in a noble and exceptionally-gifted personality. Goethe towers so markedly superior to all the other poets of culture upon German soil, that his example tests the rule.

Some of these sayings may sound hard in an age and country where culture appears to have superseded originality. They seem especially intended to discourage those of us who are doomed by the limitations of our nature to be critics, men of learning, taste, assimilation. We must comfort ourselves by reflecting that it is impossible to transcend the conditions of the times we live in, or the limits of our personality.

Society would reach something like perfection

if each individual succeeded in self-effectuation, fulfilling the law of his own nature, and being distinguished from his neighbours by some marked quality, some special accomplishment. The concord of divers instruments constitutes the music of a symphony. The blending of distinct personalities creates the finest mental and moral harmony. To some extent, of course, this result is attained wherever human beings are associated. But we suffer too much from the tyranny of majorities, the oppression of custom, the gregarious instinct of commonplace and timid persons. As I have already tried to demonstrate, true culture tends to the differentiation of individualities, by enabling people to find out what they are made for, what they can do best, what their deepest self requires for its accomplishment. True culture is never in a condescending attitude. It knows that no kind of work, however trivial, ought to be regarded with contempt. People who carve cherry-stones, dance ballets, turn rondeaux, are as much needed as those who till the soil, construct Cabinets, or fabricate new theories of the universe. True culture respects hand-labour upon equal terms with brain-labour, the mechanic with the inventor of machinery, the critic of poetry with the singer of poems, the actor with the playwright. The world wants all sorts, and wants each sort to be of the best quality. True culture knows that the quality cannot be first-rate when the species is looked down upon. On the other hand, false culture, the kind against which Walt Whitman prophesies, encourages the growth of prigs who despise folk because they do not pursue some branch of industry which is conventionally regarded as being higher in the scale than others. It makes Pharisees, who feel themselves superior to their neighbours, because these people do not belong to their own set, their own coterie, their own creed, and so forth.

The liberality and width of toleration upon which I am insisting as signs of true culture do not imply a facile acquiescence in every doctrine or in every mode of living. True culture does not prevent a man from being pugnacious, ready to fight for his opinions, eager to conquer in what he regards as the right cause. In the universal symphony strife is no less important than concord. Fully developed personalities cannot co-exist and energise together without clash and conflict. Innovation works with conservatism, powers of revolution and of progress combine with stationary or retrogressive forces, to keep the organism in a state of active energy. As Empedocles put it, both Love and Hate are necessary to the balance of the cosmic sphere. Culture prepares us to acquiesce in this state of things as part of the universal order. While recognising our own right and duty to struggle for the truth as we perceive it, we acknowledge the same right and the same duty in our opponents. For some reason hidden from our mortal ken the world was meant to be so governed. Phenomenal existence is in a perpetual state of becoming; becoming implies cohesion and dissolution; both processes involve contention. All the soldiers in all the armies, if they act with energy, sincerity, disinterested loyalty, serve one Lord and Master.

There is, therefore, no reason to fear that the higher culture should involve men in supercilious indifference, or cynical acceptance, or the Buddhistic inertia of contemplation.

SOME NOTES ON FLETCHER'S "VALENTINIAN"

I THINK it was Mr. Swinburne who said that Beaumont and Fletcher invented the Heroic Romance. This is an acute remark, the right understanding of which will enable us to place these dramatists in their proper relation to the best art of the Elizabethan age. There seems to be no reason, in the case of their most interesting serious plays, why the climax should not be quite other than it is. We cannot conceive of *Hamlet* being brought to a fortunate conclusion for all parties, or of a tragic catastrophe being found for *The Tempest*. But if *The Maid's Tragedy* had ended happily, while *Philaster* or *A King and No King* had taken a disastrous turning in the last scenes, little violence would have been done to our sense of artistic propriety. The reason of this is that the conduct of the drama in each case is not properly tragic or properly comic, but romantic. In other words, these authors did not write plays for the sake of a well-wrought plot, or with a clear sense of the inevitable in human circumstance, or with the view of interpreting character, but for the development of an attractive tale. The tale itself is often in a true sense heroic; and though *Philaster* and *A King and No King* have happy endings, while *The Maid's Tragedy* ends unhappily, all three plays belong precisely to one and the same species—the species of heroic fable dramatically set forth by dialogue in acts and scenes.

Beaumont and Fletcher—if we may still be allowed to use these names for the work of many hands which bears their superscription—were not dramatists so much as great dramatic rhetoricians. There is dramatic rhetoric, as there is poetical rhetoric. The latter differs from true poetry in this, that it diffuses where it should condense, that it approaches the object from outside by description instead of penetrating to its core; and also that it is not inevitable, not absolutely sincere. Dramatic rhetoric has the same leading qualities. The dramatic rhetorician rarely knows how to be succinct, how to let his personages reveal themselves by actions and unconscious utterances, how to evolve his plot without explaining it by declamation put into their mouths. Furthermore, he is careless of consistency and truth to nature in the drawing of his characters, incapable of making us feel certain that so, and so only, could they have spoken, acted, looked, and moved.

Both these kinds of rhetoric, the poetical and the dramatic, form the strength of Beaumont and Fletcher. When we have once yielded ourselves up to the control of what is confessedly less potent than the truest dramatic inspiration and the highest poetry, we shall acknowledge that their rhetoric possesses a real charm. And what is more, it suits their choice of the romantic rather than the strictly tragic or comic method. While reading them, we experience the pleasure that attends impassioned improvisation, the pleasure that Bandello's audience perhaps enjoyed in listening to his pathetic and extravagant *novelle*. Thought, feeling, sentiment, language, metre ; all the elements of their art are fluid, copious, untrammelled, poured forth from a richly abundant vein. But the dramatic tension is comparatively slack, and the poetic touch comparatively tame.

No other playwrights of the epoch possessed this power of rhetoric so fully. It is the distinction of Shakespeare that, both as a poet and a dramatist, he was free from its defects and did not need its qualities ; and this in a lesser degree may be said of Webster also. Ben Jonson, in his strength and his weakness, is so far removed from Beaumont and Fletcher that we can hardly compare them. He has not the same power to fascinate; but he has far more power to impress and subjugate our mind. He takes hold of us by means of a quite different faculty, the faculty of intellectual vigour, intense cerebration, masculine grasp, artistic purpose firmly conceived and conscientiously pursued. It would be rather with Massinger, Shirley, Ford, that Beaumont and Fletcher should be matched as rhetoricians of the drama; and I think that by fulness, richness, and variety of this particular gift, the twin playwrights would easily bear off the prize.

One of the marked points about Beaumont and Fletcher's manner, in connection with their rhetoric, is that they worked like Rossini and the later masters of the Italian opera. I mean, they wrote out, at full, all the florid *fioriture* which the age required for dramatic effect, and left no iota of it to the actor's personality and gesture. They put into the actor's lips every *nuance* of the situation, so that he had nothing to do but to recite volubly what they had copiously versified. As is the case with Rossini's melodies, so with their rhetorical motives, there is not quite the pith and substance to render this method enduringly attractive. Shakespeare makes us feel men and women, talking, acting ; Beaumont and Fletcher make us feel them being talked for, provided with fluent utterance to describe their action. What partially blinded contemporaries and critics like Dryden to Shakespeare's supremacy, was that he was contented to adopt the Romantic style as it had been created by his predecessors; and his immediate successors were as yet incapable of discerning the whole difference between his use of it and Beaumont's or Fletcher's. They could perceive Jonson's superiority more easily because his elaborate performances were in a sharply contrasted style.

What I have termed dramatic rhetoric, as opposed to genuine dramatic poetry, betrayed Beaumont and Fletcher into their most serious faults as playwrights. Its want of absolute sincerity led them to violate truth, propriety, and probability, both in their fables and their characters. Sudden and unaccountable conversions to good from evil, and *vice versâ*, like Hippolyta's in *The Custom of the Country*, or Boroski's in *The Loyal Subject*; inexplicable reconcilements at the ends of plays, the most infamous people being taken into favour and pardoned, like Frederick in *A Wife for a Month;* mere tricks to deceive the audience and prepare a surprise, like Polydore's feigned death in *The Mad Lover;* all these devices to protract a plot or to wind up a story, to amuse or to astonish, at the expense of ethical and artistic fitness, belong to rhetoric, which is unconscientious in the use of means, and indifferent to the necessity of preparing effects by proper and natural gradations. To the same cause may be ascribed their almost invariable habit of overdoing moral situations. They make brave generals, like Memnon in *The Mad Lover*, proclaim their own valour in language which would be exaggerated on the lips of a panegyrist. Their virtuous women vaunt their chastity in language which suggests familiarity with the brothel. Thus, too, they cannot refrain from "volleys of execrations and defiances," cannonades of protestations. What French critics call *emphase* is for ever spoiling the effect of their most passionate scenes. It seems that they were compelled to surcharge each motive by inability to exhibit the motive clearly and precisely. They resemble those imperfect writers who expand a paragraph because they have not force, concision, mental pithiness enough to say their say in a sentence.

A more legitimate field for the display of dramatic rhetoric, and one to which they were extremely partial, is casuistry. Upon honour, chastity, loyalty, marriage, upon the right and wrong of duelling, upon the advantages and disadvantages of travel, and so forth *ad infinitum*, their discussions are luminous and eminently interesting. They succeed in debating dramatically without falling into the forensic tone which spoils this kind of casuistry in Euripides. Their characters, however they may spit fire and belch forth fury, seldom condescend to nagging.

Their true strength was shown in planning some elaborate situation, like the finale of an opera act, carefully prepared, long drawn-out, introducing the main agents of the drama. These situations are always set forth with admirable but prolix oratory. Into the full effect of such dramatic climaxes, we, who only read them, can but dimly see. They must have intoxicated an audience whose eyes were satiated with the groupings of practised actors, and whose ears were delighted with the declamation of honeyed eloquence. That audience hardly perceived the thinness of the stream of poetry, the oftentimes miserable absurdity of the plot, or the occasional impropriety of the part assigned to a chief character. The sustained psychological coherence and the perfection of single scenes, in which Shakespeare had no rival, were hardly missed by them. They were fascinated by the linked sweetness of Beaumont's verbal music, by the glitter of his rapidly changing lights and shadows of emotion. Furthermore, they were warmed with passion, and the passion, though diluted, was vehement and various. They were interested in casuistical questions and scruples of honour, analogous to those which their own lives yielded. They were touched and melted by sentiment and romance, beyond the scope perhaps of their experience, but yet upon the plane of their habitual attitude toward life.

All these considerations taken together go far to explain why the attractive and many-coloured, but essentially inferior dramatic work of Beaumont and Fletcher took so strong a hold upon the imagination of the age as almost to eclipse the fame of Shakespeare. Not only in regard to casuistry, but also in many other points, it might be compared with that of the great Greek dramatic rhetorician Euripides; and we know that Euripides, though the least excellent, was for centuries the most popular of the three Attic tragedians.

The tragedy which I have selected to illustrate these general remarks is one that may with safety be attributed to the sole hand of Fletcher, and which ranks among the finest of his compositions. Founded upon actual events in the life of Valentinian III., it presents the facts of history in a romantic spirit, partly in order to increase the interest of the fable, and partly to secure unity for what would otherwise have been a disjointed plot. The principal actors in the drama are Valentinian and his wife Eudoxia, the Roman general Aëcius, Maximus and his wife Lucina, together with a crowd of servile creatures, male and female, used by the Emperor in his pleasures and addicted basely to his service. For the furtherance of the action, Fletcher has introduced some Roman soldiers, of no historical importance; detailed allusion to whom is not here necessary.

The first act, as is common with the more skilful craftsmen of the great English period, blocks out the plot with masterly precision. In the first scene a dialogue between Valentinian's four base Ministers lays bare the character of the Emperor, and unfolds the plot which he has laid for Lucina. The second scene introduces Lucina herself, and shows with what constancy she resists the flatteries and blandishments of the court ladies sent to corrupt her mind. Only, in depicting this Roman ideal of matronal chastity, Fletcher, with his wonted coarseness of taste, has touched on very slippery ground. Balbus, it is true, reports that when he hinted in her ears how easily the Emperor might play the part of Tarquin to her:

> *She pointed to a Lucrece that hung by,*
> *And with an angry look, that from her eyes*
> *Shot vestal fire against me, she departed.*

This is fine. But upon Lucina's own lips the dramatist ought never to have put such words of double meaning as the following, addressed to Phorba and Ardelia—

> *I perceive ye:*
> *Your own dark sins dwell with ye! and that price*
> *You sell the chastity of modest wives at,*
> *Run to diseases with your bones!*

In the third scene we learn the characters of Maximus and Aëcius, and their several dispositions toward the Emperor sunk in his vices. Maximus is hot with indignation, excusing the disaffection of the nation and the mutinous spirit of the army by Valentinian's own intolerable conduct. Aëcius, who suffers no less deeply on account of the degradation of the empire, preserves his loyalty intact. The high-flown conception of kinghood which marks the Jacobean drama finds noble expression in this speech:—

> *Yet remember,*
> *We are but subjects, Maximus; obedience*
> *To what is done, and grief for what is ill done,*
> *Is all we can call ours. The hearts of princes*
> *Are like the temples of the gods; pure incense,*
> *Until unhallowed hands defile those offerings,*
> *Burns ever there; we must not put 'em out,*
> *Because the priests that touch those sweets are*
> *   wicked;*

> *We dare not, dearest friend, nay, more, we cannot,—*
> *Whilst we consider who we are, and how,*
> *To what laws bound, much more to what lawgiver;*
> *Whilst majesty is made to be obeyed,*
> *And not inquired into; whilst gods and angels*
> *Make but a rule as we do, though a stricter,—*
> *Like desperate and unseasoned fools, let fly*
> *Our killing angers, and forsake our honours.*

Valentinian himself is next brought in view, hearing from the lips of Aëcius what the soldiers say against him, the peril of his throne, and the unworthy part which he is playing on the world's stage. There is no want of candour now in the old general, who had lately spoken with such submissive reverence of the divinity that doth hedge a king. Fletcher draws this Emperor as rather weak than utterly bad; he is a lawless young man with the making of a tyrant in him.

The first act having thus presented the chief characters and outlined the plot, the second act brings on the business of the play. Valentinian gains at dice the ring of Maximus, by means of which he intends to bring Lucina to the palace, and there to effect forcibly what the arts of his sycophants have failed to compass. The second and third scenes are employed in throwing further light upon Lucina, who goes unwillingly to court at the exhibition of her husband's ring, and in developing the situation between Valentinian, his generals, and the half-rebellious army.

Scenes 4, 5, and 6 of act ii. and scene 1 of act iii. are closely linked together in one rhythm of imaginative presentation; all the emotions of thrilling expectation, pathos, tragic passion, and profound pity being successively called forth, and verbally expressed with the dramatic rhetoric which I have qualified as the chief note of Fletcher's art. It is a very masterly example of his power to sustain a carefully prepared situation, and to prolong its interest by the gradual heightening of romantic incident. In the first of these connected scenes Lucina enters the great hall of the palace, attended by her two waiting women, and received by Chilax. In the next she passes to an inner apartment, still more sumptuous, where two of Fletcher's sweetest lyrics, sung to music, greet her ears. Lovely as are these songs in themselves, they possess a peculiar and almost plaintive beauty in their dramatic context; for never surely was the seductiveness of wanton pleasure more airily and delicately insinuated:

> *Now the lusty spring is seen;*
> *Golden yellow, gaudy blue,*
> *Daintily invite the view.*
> *Everywhere on every green,*

> *Roses blushing as they blow,*
> *And enticing men to pull;*
> *Lilies whiter than the snow,*
> *Woodbines of sweet honey full:*
> *All love's emblems, and all cry,*
> *"Ladies, if not plucked, we die."*

Then again :

> *Hear, ye ladies that despise*
> *What the mighty Love hath done;*
> *Fear examples, and be wise;*
> *Fair Calisto was a nun;*
> *Leda, sailing on the stream*
> *To deceive the hopes of man,*
> *Love accounting but a dream,*
> *Doted on a silver swan;*
> *Danaë, in a brazen tower,*
> *Where no love was, loved a shower.*

But Lucina, when she is asked how she likes the song, only replies :

> *I like the air well;*
> *But for the words, they are lascivious,*
> *And over-light for ladies.*

Then Balbus displays a heap of jewels, thrown about in rich profusion, for her acceptance. She passes them by, and going forward, is met by Valentinian's ladies strewing rushes in her honour :—

> *Where is this stranger? Rushes, ladies, rushes!*
> *Rushes as green as summer for this stranger!*

At this point the men retire, her waiting-women are withdrawn, and Lucina has perforce to accept the proffered hospitality of the court dames. They take her onward into a third chamber, where the door closes on her; and when again it opens, Valentinian appears to the sound of soft music, leading her by the hand, and advancing up the stage, alone with her at last. Now she knows, what she had always feared, that the ring of Maximus has been used as a lure to bring her to her ruin. She pleads for her honour, appealing to the sacredness of Cæsar, to her husband's services, kneeling upon the ground to crave for pity:

> *You are Cæsar,*
> *Which is, "the father of the empire's honour";*
> *You are too near the nature of the gods*
> *To wrong the weakest of all creatures, women.*

But prayers are vain, and when this act closes we know that poor Lucina's doom will be accomplished.

There are few instances of dramatic rhetoric finer than the succession of these three scenes, ascending to a tragic climax through so many stages of preparation. It may, however, be questioned whether the full effect was realised on the London stage in the first years of the seventeenth century, for there everything was left to the imagination; and though the purest dramatic poetry gains rather than it loses by simplicity of presentation, what I have called dramatic rhetoric is specially adapted to magnificence of *mise en scène.* In one of our great modern theatres, the Scala at Milan, for example, a proper spectacular gradation might be obtained by means of drop-scenes raised successively, until, in the last scene, the whole stage lay open to its depth, and Valentinian, entering with Lucina from the bottom, should advance to the footlights for their dialogue. This device, and this alone it seems to me, could visibly convey the impression of Lucina's passage from room to room through the sinful splendours of the palace, surrounded by meretricious enticements to the ear and eye, beleaguered by the false blandishments of men and women bent on her destruction, until at last she is left alone with her all-powerful betrayer—an impression which, in reading the play, is almost overpowering.

The interval between acts ii. and iii. suffices for the deed of darkness done in some secluded chamber. When the curtain rises again, we learn from the lips of Proculus and Chilax that all is over, and are prepared for Valentinian's re-entrance with Lucina. Her tone of pleading is now changed to one of grave rebuke and fiery accusation. Fortunately for Fletcher's fame, in this difficult passage he has just avoided his usual temptation to make a heroine scold or utter things beneath her dignity. He came very near so doing, however, as will be seen from the following quotations. Lucina's first words are—

> *As long as there is motion in my body,*
> *And life to give me words, I'll cry for justice!*

In answer to this speech Fletcher found for Valentinian the strongest line in the whole play, a line which, for dramatic intensity, might be classed with some of those keen, pungent single lines in Webster and Tourneur:

> *Justice shall never hear you; I am justice.*

Then she breaks out:

> *Wilt thou not kill me, monster, ravisher?*
> *Thou bitter bane o' th' empire; look upon me,*
> *And if thy guilty eyes dare see these ruins*
> *Thy wild lust hath laid level with dishonour,*
> *The sacrilegious razing of this temple,*
> *The mother of thy black sins would have blushed at,*
> *Behold, and curse thyself! The gods will find thee,*
> *(That's all my refuge now,) for they are righteous.*
> *Vengeance and horror circle thee! The empire,*
> *In which thou liv'st a strong continued surfeit,*
> *Like poison will disgorge thee; good men raze thee*
> *For ever being read again but vicious;*
> *Women and fearful maids make vows against thee;*
> *Thy own slaves, if they hear of this, shall hate thee;*

> *And those thou hast corrupted, first fall from thee;
> And, if thou let'st me live, the soldier,
> Tired with thy tyrannies, break through obedience
> And shake his strong steel at thee!*

The accent of rhodomontade and railing, the *emphase* of which I spoke, is felt here; but, notwithstanding this, Lucina's abuse compares favourably with that of Bonduca, Edith in *Rollo*, and Evadne in *The Maid's Tragedy*. It was not likely that Valentinian should be moved by that; he makes, on the contrary, cynical avowals of his satisfaction and ample promises for the future, sustaining his imperial dignity with sentences like these:

> *Know I am far above the faults I do,
> And those I do, I am able to forgive too.*

Then, finding her still "cold as crystal," he leaves the wronged woman face-downward on a couch, where she is discovered by her husband and Aëcius, who have meanwhile come to court.

The thread of dramatic interest, already spun to such a length, is now prolonged upon a finer and more thrilling chord of tension. The two generals extract from Lucina, by signs and mute avowals rather than by spoken words, what has happened, and learn that she is resolved to die like Lucrece. Maximus says little to break this resolution; and with tender farewells to the wretched lady, dignified in her humiliation, they send her home to perish. One of the most touching of those melodious passages, which Coleridge called Fletcher's "lyrical interbreathings," occurs here in a speech by Maximus:

> Go, Lucina;
> Already in thy tears I have read thy wrong,
> Already found a Cæsar: go, thou lily,
> Thou sweetly-drooping flower! Go, silver swan,
> And sing thine own sad requiem! Go, Lucina,
> And, if thou darest, outlive this wrong.

Aëcius now remains with his friend, striving to temper a mood that verges upon madness; and while they are thus occupied, Lucina's waiting-woman enters with the news that she has died of grief.

> When first she entered
> Into her house, after a world of weeping,
> And blushing like the sunset, as we saw her:
> "Dare I," said she, "defile this house with whore,
> In which his noble family has flourished?"
> At which she fell, and stirred no more. . . . .

That is only just passable. For Fletcher's sake let us refrain from suggesting any comparison with Giovanni's words on his mother's death in *Vittoria Corombona*. Yet it must be admitted that he has shown more reserve than is usual with him throughout the scene. Few words are wasted either by Aëcius or Maximus upon a fact which needs no amplification to enforce its pathos.

Lucina's death cuts the tragedy of Valentinian in half. The second part exhibits Fletcher's weakness as a dramatic poet. He has only arrived at the commencement of the third act, and he is bound, according to his own conception of the playwright's art, to carry the story forward without allowing the interest of the audience to cool. But he has already exhausted his finest vein of romantic poetry, and has displayed his force as a rhetorical dramatist in its fullest vigour through the long-drawn *scena* of Lucina's betrayal and heartbroken death. In continuation of the previous motive, it is true that he will have to bring poetical justice down upon the Emperor; but this is insufficient for a five-act tragedy. Therefore he begins to develop a new series of exciting incidents out of the character of Maximus. Hitherto we have known Maximus only as a bluff soldier, less tolerant than his wise and world-worn friend Aëcius towards the vices of Valentinian. He must now be employed, first through the natural passion of revenge, and afterwards through the superadded passion of a vulgar ambition, to supply a secondary motive for the plot, which otherwise would languish. It is the doom of Fletcher as a dramatic rhetorician, lacking the genuine dramatic inspiration, that he cannot convince us of the necessity of what ensues from the evolution of these two passions in the previously uncoloured character of the protagonist Maximus.

History supplied the playwright with the following events. Valentinian III. murdered the general Aëcius with his own hand, then outraged the wife of Petronius Maximus, and finally was killed by the orders of Maximus, who, after this assassination, assumed the imperial purple, and compelled Valentinian's widow, Eudoxia, to become his consort. Fletcher, in order to give unity to his plot, inverted the order of these incidents. He sought the main tragic motive in the outrage upon Lucina and the revenge of Maximus; but wishing to combine this with the murder of Aëcius, he resorted to the expedient of making Maximus the treacherous instigator of that crime. Aëcius, represented as the bosom friend of Maximus, stands in the way of his vengeance, for Maximus well knows that nothing will induce the loyal general to sanction an attempt upon the Emperor's person. He therefore flings love and honour to the winds, and forges a letter which rouses Valentinian's suspicions against his faithful subject. Aëcius, after scenes of protracted Roman eloquence, falls on his own sword, and

FLETCHER'S "VALENTINIAN" 237

when he is dead Maximus, playing a part similar to that of Antony in *Julius Cæsar*, induces Aretus and Phidias, the great general's lieutenants, to revenge his death on Valentinian. They succeed in administering poison to the Emperor, having secured an honourable exit out of life for themselves by suicide. Fletcher obviously put forth all his strength to make the scene of Valentinian's death in agony, taunted by Aretus, terrific. But those who are curious to compare dramatic rhetoric with true dramatic intensity should read that scene side by side with Brachiano's death-scene in *Vittoria Corombona*, and with the last speeches of Shakespeare's *King John*. Valentinian screams in his torment:

> *Oh, gods, gods! Drink, drink! Colder, colder*
> *Than snow on Scythian mountains! Oh, my*
>   *heart-stings!*
> *Danubius I'll have brought thorough my body,*
> *And Volga on whose face the north wind freezes.*
> *I am an hundred hells! an hundred piles*
> *Already to my funeral are flaming!*
> *Shall I not drink? . . . . . .*
>   *. . . . . . By Heaven!*
> *I'll let my breath out, that shall burn ye all,*
> *If ye deny me longer! Tempests blow me,*
> *And inundations that have drunk up kingdoms,*
> *Flow over me and quench me!*

These frenzies, put together from successive

speeches, are striking. But they will not stand beside King John's:

> There is so hot a summer in my bosom
> That all my bowels crumble up to dust;
> I am a scribbled form, drawn with a pen
> Upon a parchment, and against this fire
> Do I shrink up. . . . .
> Poisoned—ill fare ;—dead, forsook, cast off;
> And none of you will bid the winter come,
> To thrust his icy fingers in my maw;
> Nor let my kingdom's rivers take their course
> Through my burn'd bosom; nor entreat the north
> To make his bleak winds kiss my parched lips,
> And comfort me with cold.

After all these deaths, Maximus reflects upon the general ruin he has wrought. His thirst for vengeance has been satisfied, but at the expense of his friend's betrayal and murder, and by the sacrifice of two brave Romans more. It is necessary to rehabilitate him in the opinion of the audience; and this Fletcher feebly attempts to do by making him express a rhetorical desire to join Lucina and Aëcius in Elysium. That, however, is but mere bravado; and his next thought is how to grasp the empire. He secures the good-will of the army, and then prevails upon Eudoxia to become his wife, pretending that he has waded through treason, treachery, and murder—nay, the undoing of Lucina also—to the throne for love of her. She submits in appearance, and at a great public banquet crowns him with the imperial wreath. But the wreath is poisoned, and he dies amid the acclamations of " Hail, Cæsar!" with the Bacchic melodies of " God Lyæus, ever young," sounding in his ears.

The incurable fault of *Valentinian* as a tragedy is now apparent. It lies in the inadequate motives provided by the action of Maximus after Lucina's death. Up to that date, Fletcher had suggested nothing in his character which prepares us for the fraud he works on Aëcius in order to secure his revenge; and no sooner have we condoned that baseness on the hypothesis that grief had maddened him, than we are asked to accept the intrusion of ambition into his nature, and the outrageous indecency of his feigned avowals to Eudoxia, with even less of explanation. In one word, Maximus, upon whom the whole conduct of the drama turns, has been wantonly and cynically used as a mere machine for evolving a succession of stirring scenes. The romantic playwright, the rhetorical dramatist, is content to sacrifice psychological coherence, probability, and the facts of history for the sake of a magnificent but insufficiently developed series of effects.

It would be unfair to stigmatize Beaumont and Fletcher as the only, or indeed as the chief, sinners in this respect among our early playwrights. When the English drama settled into its romantic form, after the attempts made by the authors of *Gorboduc* and others to mould it on a classical type, it was already committed to the dramatisation of stories; and stories, so long as they presented striking situations and a fable of exciting interest, were welcomed without due regard for their artistic suitableness to tragic presentation. In an Italian *novella*, ill-developed motives and psychological incoherences of all sorts were excusable or passed unnoticed, the narrator dealing lightly with his material, and holding the attention of his audience only for the brief space of half an hour or so. But these defects, when transferred to the exacting sphere of the drama, which demands more detailed working out of character and a firmer grasp upon causation, became glaringly apparent, and formed the main source of weakness in the tragedies of nearly all our playwrights. It is because Beaumont and Fletcher possessed such brilliant gifts in rich abundance, and because they adorned their romances with such delightful eloquence, falling only just short of the higher poetry and the more poignant dramatic imagination, that I have submitted the composite work which passes under their joint names to a seemingly severe criticism.

THE LYRISM OF THE ENGLISH ROMANTIC DRAMA

THE most prominent feature of the English Romantic or Elizabethan Drama is a predominance of high-strung poetry in all its parts. When we compare this drama with that of Italy or of France at the same epoch, or even with that of Athens in the classical period, its characteristic quality is found to be a diffusion of lyrical poetry through every fibre, vein, and tissue of its vital structure.

The conception of character and the choice of situations in our drama are always poetical. Imagination never fails, even when the construction of the plot is lamentably defective. The playwright, in his diction, in his images and metaphors, in his rhetorical embroidery, in his handling of blank-verse, exhibits a poetic faculty which sometimes conceals the poverty of his dramatic resources. It often happens that the effect of dialogue or soliloquy is dramatically weakened by the abundance of imagery and the wealth of fancy lavished by the poet. The tone of diction proper to dramatic utterance frequently exhales in lyrisms. These "lyrical interbreathings," as Coleridge called them with admirable nicety of phrase, are exquisitely charming. To the student in his chamber they offer new delights at every turning of the page. They appeal to his imagination; they stimulate his sense of beauty and of passion in the outer and the inner worlds of nature and mankind. But they tend to clog and interrupt the business of the scene. In the hands of playwrights of the second order, of Fletcher for example, these "lyrical interbreathings," constantly repeated, degenerate into a kind of poetical rhetoric, which excuses or cloaks a want of dramatic sincerity, a feeble grasp on the essential conditions of character and action.

The lyrical element, which I have attempted to describe, was not peculiar to the drama. It pervaded all species of poetry in the Elizabethan age. That was the time when music flourished in England. We had then a native school of composers, and needed not to borrow the melodies of other lands. Every house had its lute suspended on the parlour-wall. In every company of men and women part-songs could be sung. When poets sat down to write, music sounded in their ears. Their thoughts and rhythms moved instinctively to vocal tunes. Thus we find that the epical, narrative, and meditative verse of the period, no less than the dramatic, was penetrated with lyrism. Many of the finest passages in the *Faery Queen* seem written to be sung. The lyric cry is audible throughout Marlowe's *Hero and Leander;* not only in its high uplifted passion, but also in the tense and quivering movement of the lines. Shakespeare's sonnets are lyrical, both in their structure and their tone. In this respect they differ from the sonnets of Milton, where the gnomic or reflective element predominates.

The dramatists, not unnaturally, felt this lyric impulse. It is the function of the drama in all ages to reflect the very form and pressure of the time in which it flourishes. The material conditions of the English theatre were also favourable to the development of a lyrical element in our drama. In the absence of scenery or stage-decorations appeal had to be made to the imagination of the spectators. That was done by raising the accent of poetic speech to such a pitch that the wildest flights of fancy emphasized the playwright's meaning. There were only men and boys upon the wooden platform of the stage. What these actors uttered had to bring distant scenes within the vision of the audience; their lines interpreted subtle changes of emotion, sudden reverses of fortune, the flux and reflux of passion in human hearts; and all this had to be presented with nothing but a bare background, with the open sky above, with people in hats and trunk-hose sitting, smoking, jostling the players on the stage. That being so, it is not wonderful that the playwright used the lyric note, the note of high impassioned poetry, to stimulate the fancy of his audience, and to carry them away with him into the realm of the ideal. He could not act upon their sense of sight, as the modern playwright does. Unless he pierced their intellectual sense, he failed to rivet their attention. It is thus, at any rate, that I partly explain to myself the lyrism of the English drama.

In plain words, the bias of poetical literature in England during the Elizabethan age was lyrical. The drama obeyed that bias. And the conditions of the London stage favoured a style of writing for the theatre which was eminently lyrical.

We see this in Marlowe, the founder of our theatre. Those famous "lunes" of *Tamburlaine*, those descants upon beauty, those apostrophes to divine Xenocratë, those fierce forth-stretchings after universal empire, are lyrical: lyrical not only in their tone and sentiment, but also in the form and exaltation of the verses which express them. The serious part of *Faustus* is a sustained lyric. The philosopher in his study evokes the image of

> *Women, or unwedded maids,*
> *Shadowing more beauty in their airy brows*
> *Than have the white breasts of the queen of love.*

He cries to the fiend who buys and sells him :

> *Had I as many souls as there be stars,*
> *I'd give them all for Mephistophilis.*

When Helen appears to him in a vision, he exclaims :

> *Was this the face that launched a thousand ships,*
> *And burned the topless towers of Ilium ?—*
> *Sweet Helen, make me immortal with a kiss—*
> *O, thou art fairer than the evening air*
> *Clad in the beauty of a thousand stars ;*
> *Brighter art thou than flaming Jupiter*
> *When he appeared to hapless Semelë ;*
> *More lovely than the monarch of the sky*
> *In wanton Arethusa's azured arms ;*
> *And none but thou shalt be my paramour !*

The lyrical accent here is unmistakable. Preserving the form of dramatic verse, keeping well to his decasyllabic metre, Marlowe soars aloft into that higher region of poetry where music is demanded. He does not rely upon the decoration or the business of the stage : he forces the audience, by poetry, by the evocation of their sympathies, by a keen lyric cry, to comprehend the dramatic situation.

If we abstract the lyrical passages from *Tamburlaine* and *Faustus* there remains but little noteworthy in these plays. The case is different with *Edward II*. Here Marlowe constructs a tragedy, which would be forcibly dramatic without its lyrical element. The lyrism survives. It is particularly potent in the scene of Edward's abdication. But the action and the passions move almost without its help. The lyric, which was nearly everything in *Tamburlaine* and *Faustus*, has become a subordinate quantity in *Edward II*.

At the point which Marlowe reached in *Edward II.*, Shakespeare took his art up. Shakespeare always regarded the dramatic movement of the play first. But he never neglected the lyrical element. He recognised this as a main point in the romantic drama, which he was born to perfect. And he has more than once or twice written plays which are purely lyrical in their construction.

It will suffice to mention *Romeo and Juliet*. This is a lyrical poem, dramatically presented. As a German critic has remarked, *Romeo and Juliet* combines the sonnet, the epithalamium, and the aubade—three types of lyrical poetry—under one dramatic form. The whole play is a *Chant d'Amour*—an exhalation of human love, in poetry assuming the dramatic mantle. All the incidents of action fall away and sink into their place before the simple fact that Romeo loves Juliet, and Juliet loves Romeo. This play is the lyric cry converted into drama.

It would be easy to show by copious illustrations how lyrically conceived and executed is the tragedy of *Richard II*. Nor would it be difficult to point out in what way *Love's Labour's Lost* falls short of being a good comedy by its dependence upon lyrical rhymed structures in the metre, and by its incongruous admixture of high lyric flights of passion—Biron's ecstatic extravaganzas—with satirical humour and frank buffoonery. This play, in some respects one of the most charming of Shakespeare's earliest efforts, closing as it does upon the note of one of his most genial and native songs, does not indeed deserve the name of a comedy, but rather that of some ethereal variety-entertainment, because of its imperfectly assimilated lyrism. Far more finely mingled are the elements of comedy and lyric in *A Midsummer Night's Dream*, which is really a dramatic romance, interweaving three separate strains of poetry—the heroic in Theseus, the amorous in the two pairs of lovers, the fantastic in the fairies—with one strain of burlesque, toned exquisitely into keeping with the major parts. I should like lastly to demonstrate how *The Tempest*, a work of Shakespeare's maturity, is a pure ideal lyric, converted by the master's wonder-working wand into an effective drama for the stage, without the sacrifice of its dominant quality, but rather by the maintenance of the lyric note throughout. Descending to the compositions of minor playwrights, it is enough to mention Dekker's *Old Fortunatus*, Day's *Parliament of Bees*, Fletcher's *Faithful Shepherdess*, and many of the later romantic tragi-comedies, in which the lyrism of the English drama is most noticeable.

Marlowe proved in *Edward II.* that a tragedy could be constructed, which was not dependent on its lyrical element, but which used that only for purposes of occasional rhetoric and powerful appeal to the imagination of the audience. The type which he then fixed became the standard for his immediate successors.

This brings us back to what Coleridge called the "lyrical interbreathings" of the romantic drama, and necessitates a closer examination of those portions of non-lyrical plays in which the dramatic style modulates into the lyric.

The passages in Shakespeare's tragedies and comedies where dialogue or soliloquy soars into the empyrean of impassioned poetry are so frequent, and some of them are so famous, that it is needless to do more than allude to them in passing. Macbeth's declamation on the vanity of life, when he hears the news of the Queen's death; Perdita's melodious enumeration of spring-flowers; Claudio's horror-stricken meditation on the state of disembodied spirits; the narrative of Ophelia's drowning; the last speeches of Antony and Cleopatra—especially that sublime cry of hers:

> *I am again for Cydnus,*
> *To meet Mark Antony!—*

all these illustrate what I mean by dramatic style transfigured, raised to lyrical intensity. So are some of those brief snatches which occur occasionally in almost unexpected places, as when Timon dismisses the Athenian senators:

> *Come not to me again; but say to Athens,*
> *Timon hath made his everlasting mansion*
> *Upon the beachèd verge of the salt flood;*
> *Whom once a day with his embossèd froth*
> *The turbulent surge shall cover.*

So, again, are those vignetted pictures, and freaks of roving fancy, which present an episode idealized, and strike the keynote of its purified emotion. A good instance of this is when Lorenzo and Jessica exchange their lovers' thoughts by means of musical allusions—a sustained and measured dialogue in antiphonal descant—beneath the flooding moonlight in the Park at Belmont:

> LOR. *In such a night*
> *Stood Dido with a willow in her hand*
> *Upon the wild sea banks, and waft her love*
> *To come again to Carthage.*
> JES. *In such a night*
> *Medea gathered the enchanted herbs*
> *That did renew old Aeson.*

This uplifting of dramatic into lyrical style in dialogue and soliloquy is common to all those of the Elizabethan playwrights who were gifted with a genuine poetic faculty. We find it everywhere in Fletcher's romantic plays. I need not cull examples from *The Faithful Shepherdess*, for that is obviously lyrical throughout. I will rather allude in passing to Ordella's panegyric on death in *Thierry and Theodoret;* to Memnon's address to his young mistress in *The Mad Lover;* to Aspatia's impassioned vision of Ariadne on the desert island in *The Maid's Tragedy*. These are doubtless too familiar to call for quotation in full. But a passage may be selected from *The Custom of the Country*—that comedy which might be called a dung-heap strewn with pearls—to illustrate the specific quality of Fletcher's lyrism:

> *Strew all your withered flowers, your autumn sweets,*
> *By the hot sun ravished of bud and beauty,*
> *Thus round about her bride-bed; hang these blacks there,*
> *The emblems of her honour lost: all joy*
> *That leads a virgin to receive her lover,*
> *Keep from this place; all fellow maids that bless her,*
> *And blushing do unloose her zone, keep from her;*
> *No merry noise, nor lusty songs, be heard here,*
> *Nor full cups crowned with wine make the rooms giddy:*
> *This is no masque of mirth, but murdered honour.*
> *Sing mournfully that sad epithalamion*
> *I gave thee now; and, prithee, let thy lute weep.*

We note the same ascent to lyrism in Heywood. When Mr. Frankford, in *A Woman Killed with Kindness*, is approaching and leaving his wife's bedchamber, and again when he discovers the lute which she has left behind her in the desecrated home, he breaks into soliloquies ringing with a wounded heart-cry. The intensity of the situation changes the accent of the verse. One of these three passages will serve as an example:

> *O God! O God! that it were possible*
> *To undo things done; to call back yesterday!*
> *That time could turn up his swift sandy glass*
> *To untell the days, and to redeem these hours!*

> Or that the sun
> Could, rising from the west, draw his coach back-
>   ward;
> Take from the account of time so many minutes,
> Till he had all these seasons called again,
> Those minutes, and those actions done in them,
> Even from her first offence; that I might take her
> As spotless as an angel in my arms!
> But, oh! I talk of things impossible,
> And cast beyond the moon."

It is the same with Webster, with Dekker with Ford, with Marston. Even Ben Jonson that strict master of severity in style, indulges now and then in flights of lyrism. Lovel's dissertation upon Platonic affection, in *The New Inn*, is an example; so too are the opening lines about Earinĕ in *The Sad Shepherd*.

We have now seen that the characteristic note of the English romantic drama is a predominance of high-strung poetry in all its parts. This poetry, even in the blank-verse passages, assumes a lyrical quality. But the spirit of this poetry goes farther; climbs higher; and the final point to which it soars, claims our attention next. The lyrical element, on which I have been so long insisting as the very mainspring of English romantic art, culminates and finds free expression in the songs which are scattered up and down each play. These songs cannot be regarded as occasional ditties, interpolated for the delectation of the audience. On the contrary, they strike the key-note of the playwright's style. They condense the particular emotion of the tragedy or comedy in a quintessential drop of melody. Mr. Pater has dwelt upon a single instance of this fact with his usual felicity of phrase. Speaking of the song of Mariana's page in *Measure for Measure*, he remarks that in it "the kindling power and poetry of the whole play seems to pass for a moment into an actual strain of music." The same might be said about the two songs in the second act of *As You Like it*, Ariel's songs in *The Tempest*, and all the fairy lyrics of *A Midsummer Night's Dream*. What painters call their *accent*, the *highest value* in their pictures, we find in these dramatic lyrics. It only requires a moment's reflection to perceive in how true a sense the little poems written by the dramatist for music at a certain point in his play, give the accent of his style, the highest value in his scheme of composition. This is very clear when we consider the dirges introduced by Webster into *The Duchess of Malfi* and *Vittoria Corombona*. The sombre genius of the poet, his sinister philosophy of life, the terrible gloom of his tragic motives, are epitomized in those funeral ditties. In like manner, the theme of Fletcher's *Valentinian* is accentuated by the two songs of the second act; and the whole spirit of *The Maid's Tragedy* lives in Aspatia's dirge:

> *Lay a garland on my hearse,*
>   *Of the dismal yew;*
> *Maidens, willow branches bear;*
>   *Say, I died true.*
>
> *My love was false, but I was firm*
>   *From my hour of birth.*
> *Upon my buried body lie*
>   *Lightly, gentle earth!*

Ford, though he was not one of the best lyrists of this period, managed to sublimate the motive of his tragedy, *The Broken Heart*, in three songs, "Can you paint a thought?" "Oh, no more, no more, too late," and "Glories, pleasures, pomps, delights, and ease."

This is equally true of comedies or dramatized romances. Dekker's lyrics in *The Pleasant Comedy of Patient Grissell* yield at once the purest accent of his own poetic quality and the highest value of the play in which they occur. Heywood's song, "Ye little birds that sit and sing," is the culminating point of his *Fair Maid of the Exchange*. The spirit of the man and the spirit of the work of art are both extracted and etherealized in the four stanzas of that exquisitely transparent ditty.

I have now made it clear in what way I think the songs which are scattered through our drama deserve to be carefully studied; first as the ultimate expression of that lyrism to which the romantic species in England was always tending; and secondly, as an index to the playwright's specific quality as poet.

Some of our dramatists were defective in the lyrical faculty. Their blank-verse lyrism is rather rhetorical than poetical; and their songs are mediocre. Massinger is of this sort; so, but in a less degree, is Middleton; and Shirley might be classed with them, had he not bequeathed to us the two immortal odes upon the vanity of human power and glory, from *Cupid and Death* and *The Contention of Ajax*.

Ben Jonson rarely struck the note of genuine inevitable lyric inspiration. None of the songs in his plays can be called perfect in their music. Beside being stiff through labour of the file, they are often awkward in some turn or other of expression. The best to my mind are the "Hymn to Diana," in *Cynthia's Revels*, and the "Ode to Charis," introduced from Underwoods into *The Devil is an Ass*. It may interest some of my readers to learn that the third stanza of this beautiful poem was parodied by Sir John Suckling in *The Sad One*. Jonson had written:

> *Have you seen but a bright lily grow*
>   *Before rude hands have touched it?*
> *Have marked but the fall of the snow*
>   *Before the soil hath smutched it?*
> *Have you felt the wool of the beaver,*
>   *Or swan's down ever?*
> *Or have smelt o' the bud of the brier,*
>   *Or the nard in the fire?*
> *Or have tasted the bag of the bee?*
> *O so white, O so soft, O so sweet is she!*

Suckling converted this to his own use as follows :

> *Hast thou seen the down in the air,*
>   *When wanton blasts have tossed it?*
> *Or the ship on the sea,*
>   *When ruder winds have crossed it?*
> *Hast thou marked the crocodile's weeping,*
>   *Or the fox's sleeping?*
> *Or hast thou viewed the peacock in his pride,*
>   *Or the dove by his bride,*
>   *When he courts for his lechery?*
> *Oh! so fickle, oh! so vain, oh! so false, so false*
>   *is she!*

The execution of the lyric in *Volpone*, " Come, my Celia, let us prove," is excellent. These couplets might be reckoned among Jonson's successes, did they not challenge fatal comparison with the Ode of Catullus, from which they are in part borrowed, but of which they are in no true sense an adequate translation. The song from *The Silent Woman,* " Still to be neat, still to be drest," transplanted into English from the Latin of Jean Bonnefons, deserves honourable mention; not only for its terseness and correction, but also because it plainly foreshadowed and probably helped to form the lyric style of the seventeenth century. If we may trust Drummond of Hawthornden, Jonson thought highly of his drinking-song in *The Poetaster.* It does not find a place in the best anthologies of songs from the dramatists. I shall therefore produce it here ; for it illustrates what I mean by Jonson's awkwardness of phrase ; and if he really set great store upon this little ode, it also illustrates his incapacity for just self-criticism :

> *Swell me a bowl with lusty wine,*
> *Till I may see the plump Lyæus swim*
>   *Above the brim:*
> *I drink as I would write,*
> *In flowing measure filled with flame and sprite.*

This is certainly inferior in poetry and rhythm to Fletcher's "God Lyæus ever young," and to Lyly's "O for a bowl of fat canary," which reappears improved in one of Middleton's comedies.* Beautiful lyrical extracts may be culled from Jonson's *Masques.* But these are only fragments, scattered stanzas, occasional

---

* *A Mad World, my Masters.*

flights above the poet's ordinary mood—like that fine passage from the *Queen's Masque*, prefiguring the style of Dryden's odes, which begins, "So beauty on the waters stood"—like the description of an ocean paradise in *The Fortunate Isles*, "The winds are sweet and gently blow"—like the dirge for withered spring-flowers in *Pan's Anniversary*, "Drop, drop, you violets, change your hues."* Indeed Jonson, with all his fine poetic feeling, was not sure of touch enough, nor exacting enough in his taste, to produce lyrics of a sustained excellence. The one absolutely faultless song he wrote, "Drink to me only with thine eyes," is absent from his dramatic works.

One playwright of the highest eminence, and two of the second order, Marlowe, Cyril Tourneur, and Marston, have no songs printed in their plays. This does not prove, however, that they wrote none; for publishers, at that period, were not always careful to retain the lyrics when they sent an author's plays to press. It also appears that stage-ditties were regarded as common property. In the case of Marston, stage directions are frequently given for the introduction of music and singing. But whether his own lyrics were used on those occasions cannot now be determined.

* The text of the Masque gives "Drop, drop, your violets." Since the violets are obviously addressed in the following lines, it seems to me that *your* must here be a misprint for *you*.

Marlowe had the lyrical faculty in over-measure. I have already pointed out what a large part blank-verse lyrism plays in his tragedies. It must therefore be left to conjecture whether he chose to dispense with the element of song, or whether in the printing of his plays the lyrics were omitted. In the latter case, we have suffered grievous wrong from the publishers of his dramatic works. But I am inclined to believe, from the stage-business of Marlowe's tragedies, that the detached lyric formed no portion of his scheme. Did we possess none but the original editions of Lyly's comedies, we should have to mourn the loss of those charming songs, which form the best part of Lyly's literary bequest to posterity. They were introduced by Edward Blount into the complete edition of 1632. With regard to Tourneur, there is no reason to suppose that he was incapable of writing songs superior to those of Ford, and not inferior to Webster's. The lyrisms in his blank-verse are magnificently poignantly fantastic.

Two collections of dramatic lyrics have been published in this century. The first, called *Songs from the Dramatists*, by Robert Bell, has long been out of print. The second, edited by Mr. A. H. Bullen, under the title of *Lyrics from Elizabethan Dramatists*, bears the date of 1889. These books, both of which are valuable, have a somewhat different scope and diverse merits. Mr. Bell begins earlier, and ends later. His first entries are the five lyrics from *Ralph Roister Doister*. His last are five songs from the comedies of Sheridan. Mr. Bullen starts with Lyly, and finishes with Jasper Mayne and Thomas Forde, contemporaries of Milton. Though Mr. Bell covers a larger ground, he is neither so complete nor so scholarly as Mr. Bullen. His anthology, delightful and useful as it is, bears the air of *dilettante* reading and caprice. Mr. Bullen is well-nigh exhaustive within the limits he has assigned to himself. He has also reproduced for the first time many interesting pieces which were known to few but specialists. I may mention, in particular, the lyrics of Thomas Nash, all of which are well worth study; of Peter Hausted, William Habington, and Richard Brome, whose charming spring ditty from *The Jolly Beggars* was unaccountably omitted by Mr. Bell. It is to be hoped that future editions of this collection will incorporate those earlier pieces which we find in Bell's anthology, adding perhaps the fresh and simple April song which opens the Morality of *Lusty Juventus*.

In the next essay I propose to consider two volumes of *Lyrics from Elizabethan Song-Books*, and the works of Dr. Thomas Campion, edited by Mr. Bullen. It is interesting to compare the contents of these collections, songs written for music and not intended for the drama, with the *Lyrics from Elizabethan Dramatists*. Surveying the whole mass of poems here presented, we first observe the common note which marks them all out as the product of one period, the outcome of one national sensibility. The style throughout is the style of that Renaissance movement which took hold of England in the last quarter of the sixteenth century, and which spent its force before the restoration of the Stuarts. There is no mistaking the similarity of tone and accent in all the lyrics written during that memorable space of somewhat more than fifty years. They have a spontaneity, a bird-like freshness, an irrecoverable facility of singing, which has never been recaptured in the centuries which followed. This divine quality of careless inspiration they possess in common. But when we look closer, we find that the dramatic lyrics differ in important respects from those of the song-books. The latter are always more generic, vaguer, broader in their emotion. They were intended to be sung in every place where men and women met together for society and recreation. Consequently, their authors tuned them to what Browning called " the common chord," " the C major of this life. The songs of the dramatists, on the other hand, cannot easily be detached from their context, from the situations they were meant to accentuate. The playwrights wrote them, as I have attempted to prove, in order to give the highest value, to strike the key-note of their compositions. Perhaps we ought not to ascribe deliberate intention to the authors of these stage songs. But being penetrated with the dramatic situation, this forced them, consciously or unconsciously, to a special treatment of the lays they wrote for it. Therefore, the emotion expressed is specific, definite, connected with the particular movement and motive of the plays where they occur. It follows that the dramatic song is more intense, high-pitched, and thrilling, than the lyric meant for chamber music. There is more concentrated stuff of thought and passion directed to a single psychological moment in its poetry.

I do not wish to assert that this is invariably the case. Examples might be culled from the drama in which the song is only interpolated as a pleasing ditty. Examples, again, might be selected from Campion, in which the song seems to demand a dramatic setting. But, broadly speaking, I think that this distinction holds good.

I have treated our romantic drama from the point of view of lyric poetry, and have tried to demonstrate its constant striving after lyrical expression in the handling of blank verse, and the culmination of that effort in the songs written to illustrate certain leading motives or decisive situations of the action.

This position is confirmed when we pass from the Elizabethan to the Restoration playwrights. The Comedy of the Restoration was essentially non-lyrical; and that is equally true of its tragedy. Even in Otway we do not discover the lyrical interbreathings which were so marked a feature of Elizabethan literature. Dryden gives us plenty of robust declamation and sonorous rhetoric; but the note of his drama is not poetical. As might be expected, the songs of this period are defective in poetic feeling and fancy. Some of Congreve's have an exquisite finish, a sparkling brilliancy; but their finish and their sparkle are those of a paste diamond. Dryden wrote rough, commonplace, and tawdry lyrics for the stage. I will quote a stanza from *The Spanish Friar*, which deserves attention, not only because it exhibits the extraordinary want of charm in Dryden's stage-songs, but also because it first exemplified the metrical scheme which Swinburne adopted for his *Garden of Proserpine*:

> *Farewell, ungrateful traitor,*
> *Farewell, my perjured swain!*
> *Let never injured creature*
> *Believe a man again.*

> *The pleasure of possessing*
> *Surpasses all expressing:*
> *But 'tis too short a blessing,*
> *And love too long a pain.*

Mr. Swinburne deserves credit for having perceived the capacities of this stanza, and for constructing the silk purse of his immortal poem out of such a veritable sow's ear.

LYRICS FROM ELIZABETHAN SONG-BOOKS

THERE are epochs in the literature of nations when something resembling clairvoyance into poetry—a true instinct as to its conditions, together with the power of shaping language in accordance with this intuition—seems to be universally distributed throughout the people. Such an epoch, in the case of England, was that to which Elizabeth gave her name, although it extended in duration considerably beyond the queen's lifetime. Throughout this period we find the English singularly gifted with dramatic and lyrical genius.

The songs of the time have a freshness and a certainty of cadence, as of some bird's note. Those scattered through the drama are comparatively well known. But we have only in recent days become acquainted with the verses written for chamber-music, many of which are no less rare and beautiful.

The first collection of lyrics reprinted from old English song-books, so far as I am aware, was Mr. Thomas Oliphant's *Musa Madrigalesca*, published in 1837. It contained a liberal anthology from Byrd, Dowland, Weelkes, Morley, Wilbye, Gibbons, Ford, Vautor, and three anonymous sources—*Melismata, Pammelia, Deuteromelia*—which have been ascribed with probability to Thomas Ravenscroft. Mr. Oliphant added much curious bibliographical and biographical information, together with copious discursive notes. Yet his book is, on the whole, unsatisfactory; for the compiler exercised no critical discrimination, but admitted the veriest trash of bad translations from the Italian, side by side with exquisite gems of English composition.

Between the years 1879 and 1883 Professor Arber, to whose indefatigable industry and exact scholarship our literature is indebted for so many recovered treasures, printed entire collections of Byrd, Yonge, Campion, Rosseter, Dowland, Alison, and Wilbye.

Adhering to his fixed principles in dealing with such reprints, Arber reproduced the original texts of these old books without alteration in successive volumes of his *English Garner*.

Though accessible to students, and eminently valuable by their textual fidelity, these republications are hardly calculated to make the lyrics from the song-books widely popular. Like Oliphant's anthology, they diffused a good deal of inferior literary matter, together with much that was both admirable and new. Campion's and Rosseter's songs, in particular, opened up a mine of exquisite lyrical melody, the existence of which had been forgotten.

In 1883, Mr. W. J. Linton's collection, entitled *Rare Poems of the Sixteenth and Seventeenth Centuries*, showed what use for purely literary purposes could be made of the Elizabethan song-books. While culling pieces from eminent authors—Sidney, Jonson, Beaumont, Waller, Lovelace and Marvell—Mr. Linton drew freely upon Dowland, Byrd, Morley, Wilbye, Weelkes, Ford, Farmer, and the other sources edited by Oliphant and Arber.

It remained for Mr. A. H. Bullen to present the public with a full and critical selection of the choicest pieces. His *Lyrics from the Song-Books of the Elizabethan Age*, which appeared in 1887, resumed the labours of his predecessors, and widely extended the field of research. This volume has been followed by a second, under the same title. Not only has Mr. Bullen carefully examined and collected the song-books previously edited by Oliphant and Arber; but he has disinterred large numbers of entirely new lyrics, partly from rare copies extant in public and private libraries, partly also from MS. sources undreamed of by the ordinary student and inaccessible to nearly every one. The result is that his anthologies are, without comparison, the richest in variety of materials. But that is not their only feature. What renders them of special value from the point of view of literature, as distinguished from scholarship, is that he has employed a fine critical taste and sound judgment in making his selections. Those who shall take the trouble to compare his specimens from Byrd, Yonge, Dowland, Campion, Alison, and Wilbye, with Arber's reprints, will find that he has skimmed the cream for us, beside introducing many fresh jewels of bright and delicate lustre.

These lyrics from the song-books have not the intensity of some songs introduced into dramas of the Elizabethan period. They are rarely so high-strung and weighty with meaning as Webster's dirges, or as Ford's and Shirley's solemn descants on the transitiveness of earthly love and glory. Nor again do we often welcome in them that fulness of romantic colour, which makes the lyrics of Beaumont and Fletcher so resplendent. This is, perhaps, because their melodies are not the outgrowth of dramatic situations, but have their life and being in the more aerial element of musical sound. For the purposes of singing they are exactly adequate, being substantial enough to sustain and animate the notes, and yet so slight as not to overburden these with too much reflection and emotion. We feel that they have arisen spontaneously from the natural and facile marrying of musical words to musical phrases; they are the right and fitting verbal counterpart to vocal and instrumental melody; limpid, liquid, never surcharging the notes which need them as a vehicle with complexities of fancy, involutions of thought, or the disturbing tyranny of vehement passions. It is clear in many cases that the literary and the musical parts of these delicious compositions were begotten simultaneously. This is the right quality of song; the presence of this indicates true familiarity with musical requirements in England of the sixteenth century.

Who were the authors of these lyrics? That is a difficult question to answer. The large majority must be accepted as anonymous, or in the more delicate language of the old Greeks, as "masterless," ἀδέσποτα. It would be uncritical to assume that the composers of the music, under whose names the books were issued, always wrote their own poetry. Indeed, the contrary can sometimes easily be proved; for we find pieces by Sidney, Dyer, Drayton, and other well-known poets, set to melodies. There is, however, a strong presumption in favour of the belief that John Dowland, Robert Jones, and Thomas Campion, wrote their own words. The greatest of these men was Campion; and he has now at last, through Mr. Bullen's complete edition of his works, been restored to his right place among the first and best of English lyrists. In the preface to his *Third Book of Airs*, Campion remarks: "In these English Airs I have chiefly aimed to couple my words and notes lovingly together; which will be much for him to do that hath not power over both." I take this to be pretty conclusive proof, if other proof from the testimony of contemporaries were wanting, that Campion composed both words and notes in the pieces published under his own name. Still, we must not assume that *every* song in Campion's books belongs to him. The evidence for John Dowland's authorship is not quite so clear. Yet the identity of style presented by those "rich clusters of golden verse"—so Mr. Bullen describes the songs in Dowland's books—together with the absence from his prefaces of any reference to other writers, will justify our hailing his touch on language as no less heavenly than Richard Barnfield found his touch upon the lute to be. The songs of Robert Jones are in like manner marked by signs of an individual style, which can be best explained by supposing that he made his own verses.

When we come to classify the topics of these lyrics, it will be convenient to divide them roughly under a few headings. (1) The first group is composed of sacred ditties, hymns, invocations, prayers, psalms of repentance, and thanksgivings. (2) The second group includes little poems upon human life, of that nature which the Greeks called gnomic. Proverbial wisdom is here expressed in flowing verse. (3) The third group embraces the wide and universal theme of love. We have to subdivide it into songs of wooing supplicating love, of love triumphant and enjoyed, of sorrowing and pining love, of love rejected, of scornful and disdainful love, and lastly of light love and ephemeral flirtation. As will be readily conceived, this third group is by far the largest. Some of its lyrics are direct and poignant, arrows shot from the bow-strings of the heart in moments of unreflective feeling. Others assume the gentle affection of the pastoral style, which lends itself so prettily to musical effect. In the former, I and thou, the immortal personages of the heart's duet, sing their undying descant from the solitude of soul to soul. In the latter, Phyllis and Corydon, Thoralis and Lycidas, shepherd their flocks upon green lawns, and bend beribboned crooks to the swaying of leafy boughs in spring or summer. (4) A fourth group contains humorous songs of many sorts; some frankly comic, some fitted for drinking-bouts and tavern-company, some satirical, some trenching on the sphere of politics. (5) To a fifth group, though it is a small one, I would consign those compositions which deal with the praise of music, as an element in man's spiritual life.

It is my purpose to present a few choice specimens of these several groups in turn. I shall confine myself to Mr. Bullen's two volumes, and, where I think this possible, I shall give the author's name of each piece. These specimens must be regarded only as samples, chosen, partly at haphazard, partly through some personal sense in me of their peculiar beauty. Many of the songs which I omit to quote, will seem, in other eyes than mine, of equal or superior excellence. What Byrd wrote in the preface to his first collection of English songs, holds good in a far wider sense than he intended:—"Benign reader, here is offered unto thy courteous acceptance, music of sundry sorts, and to content divers humours." Out of the hundreds of lyrics which Mr. Bullen has selected, every man of taste and feeling will form a different anthology of fifty. That is the charm of this large river-head of song. We can all fill our own pitchers at its fount of melody, and each will be surprised to find that his neighbour has brought something different away.

From the first group, that of pious songs, I will begin by selecting one by Thomas Campion:

> *Awake, awake! thou heavy sprite*
> *That sleep'st the deadly sleep of sin!*
> *Rise now and walk the ways of light,*
> *'Tis not too late yet to begin.*
> *Seek heaven early, seek it late;*
> *True faith finds still an open gate.*
>
> *Get up, get up, thou leaden man!*
> *Thy track to endless joy or pain,*
> *Yields but the model of a span:*
> *Yet burns out thy life's lamp in vain!*
> *One minute bounds thy fame or bliss;*
> *Then watch and labour while time is.*

Another of Campion's religious pieces has the merit of simplicity and unaffected piety.

> *View me, Lord, a work of Thine!*
> *Shall I then lie drown'd in night?*
> *Might Thy grace in me but shine,*
> *I should seem made all of light.*
>
> *But my soul still surfeits so*
> *On the poison'd baits of sin,*
> *That I strange and ugly grow;*
> *All is dark and foul within*

> *Cleanse me, Lord, that I may kneel*
>   *At Thine altar pure and white:*
> *They that once Thy mercies feel,*
>   *Gaze no more on earth's delight.*
>
> *Worldly joys like shadows fade*
>   *When the heavenly light appears:*
> *But the covenants Thou hast made,*
>   *Endless, know not days nor years.*
>
> *In Thy Word, Lord, is my trust,*
>   *To Thy mercies fast I fly;*
> *Though I am but clay and dust,*
>   *Yet Thy grace can lift me high.*

Here is a scrap from the MSS. preserved at Christ Church Oxford, the metaphor of which may serve as introduction to a far nobler composition from the same source:

> *Turn in, my Lord, turn into me,*
> *My heart's a homely place;*
> *But Thou canst make corruption flee,*
> *And fill it with Thy grace:*
> *So furnishèd it will be brave,*
> *And a rich dwelling thou shalt have.*

I hardly know with what words to preface the next poem, only a fragment, alas! as it appears by the abrupt commencement. Its extreme beauty of diction and dignity of phrase, its rich and ample rhetoric, deep-coloured but subdued in tone, mark it out for the work of no mere

ELIZABETHAN SONG-BOOKS

'prentice hand in poetry. Could we think of it as Vaughan's? Its style is grander than that of Herbert, more exquisite than that of Jonson, more pompous than that of Herrick. Happy indeed was Mr. Bullen, when this jewel, luminous by reason even of the fracture which has shivered it, sparkled before his eyes among the dusty MSS. in Christ Church Library!

Yet if his majesty our sovereign lord
Should of his own accord
Friendly himself invite,
And say " I'll be your guest to morrow night,"
How should we stir ourselves, call and command
All hands to work! "Let no man idle stand.
Set me fine Spanish tables in the hall,
See they be fitted all;
Let there be room to eat,
And order taken that there want no meat.
See every sconce and candlestick made bright,
That without tapers they may give a light.
Look to the presence! are the carpets spread,
The dais o'er the head,
The cushions in the chairs,
And all the candles lighted on the stairs?
Perfume the chambers, and in any case
Let each man give attendance in his place."
Thus if the king were coming would we do,
And 'twere good reason too;
For 'tis a duteous thing
To show all honour to an earthly king,
And after all our travail and our cost,

So he be pleased, to think no labour lost.
But at the coming of the King of Heaven
All's set at six and seven:
We wallow in our sin,
Christ cannot find a chamber in the inn.
We entertain him always like a stranger,
And as at first still lodge him in a manger.

The music to these royal words was composed by Thomas Ford. I wish that we could venture to think that he wrote them. In that case Thomas Ford would rank beside his illustrious namesake, the tragic poet John Ford, as one of the finest masters of our language. He was an excellent musician, and made use of admirable lyrics. Since I have introduced this subject, I will submit two other poems which he set.

Since first I saw your face, I resolved to honour and renown ye;
If now I be disdained, I wish my heart had never known ye.
What? I that loved and you that liked, shall we begin to wrangle?
No, no, no, my heart is fast, and cannot disentangle.

If I admire or praise you too much, that fault you may forgive me;
Or if my hands had strayed but a touch, then justly might you leave me.

> *I asked your leave, you bade me love; is't now a
>   time to chide me?
> No, no, no, I'll love you still, what fortune e'er be-
>   tide me.
> The sun whose beams most glorious are, rejecteth no
>   beholder;
> And your sweet beauty past compare made my poor
>   eyes the bolder.
> Where beauty moves, and wit delights, and signs of
>   kindness bind me,
> There, O there! where'er I go, I'll leave my heart
>   behind me.*

This is in the grand style also, the style of subdued and loyal passion, deep and calm as the flow of a steady river. The next piece, again set by Ford, is in a lighter key of feeling. Yet it retains something of the superb chivalrous manner. Both emotion and diction are noble.

> *There is a lady sweet and kind;
> Was never face so pleased my mind:
> I did but see her passing by,
> And yet I love her till I die.*
>
> *Her gesture, motion, and her smiles,
> Her wit, her voice, my heart beguiles,
> Beguiles my heart, I know not why,
> But yet I love her till I die.*
>
> *Her free behaviour, winning looks,
> Will make a lawyer burn his books;
> I touched her not, alas! not I;
> And yet I love her till I die.*

> *Cupid is wingèd, and doth range;*
> *Her country so my love doth change;*
> *But change she earth, or change she sky,*
> *Yet will I love her till I die.*

If Thomas Ford really composed these three pieces of poetry which he set to music, we must henceforth look upon him as the writer of three of the most touching lyrics in our language. I will resume my selections from the religious airs in the song-books. Take this little piece from John Danyel's *Songs for the Lute, Viol and Voice,* 1606. Notice how it is steeped in the shadow of religious gloom and deep compunction.

> *If I could shut the gate against my thoughts*
>   *And keep out sorrow from this room within,*
> *Or memory could cancel all the notes*
>   *Of my misdeeds, and I unthink my sin:*
> *How free, how clear, how clean my soul should lie,*
> *Discharged of such a loathsome company!*
>
> *Or were there other rooms without my heart*
>   *That did not to my conscience join so near,*
> *Where I might lodge the thoughts of sin apart*
>   *That I might not their clam'rous crying hear;*
> *What peace, what joy, what ease should I possess,*
> *Freed from their horrors that my soul oppress!*
>
> *But, O my Saviour, who my refuge art,*
>   *Let thy dear mercies stand 'twixt them and me,*
> *And be the wall to separate my heart*
>   *So that I may at length repose me free;*
> *That peace, and joy, and rest may be within,*
> *And I remain divided from my sin.*

One of Campion's compositions, upon the border-land between pious ditties and gnomic pieces, may here be introduced. The second stanza, though impaired by a certain slightness of execution, which is not unfrequent in Campion, begins very nobly and has a high and lofty tone of feeling.

To music bent is my retirèd mind
And fain would I some song of pleasure sing,
But in vain joys no comfort now I find,
From heavenly thoughts all true delight doth spring:
Thy power, O God, thy mercies to record,
Will sweeten every note and every word.

All earthly pomp or beauty to express
Is but to carve in snow, on waves to write;
Celestial things, though men conceive them less,
Yet fullest are they in themselves of light:
Such beams they yield as know no means to die,
Such heat they cast as lifts the spirit high.

Moral and sententious poems, embodying maxims upon life, are common enough in these collections. Most of them turn upon the blessings of content, and upon the contrast between a courtier's or statesman's life and that of humble folk and peasants. The key-note is struck in that famous poem, which Sidney's friend Sir Edward Dyer is said to have written. William Byrd set it to music in 1588.

*My mind to me a kingdom is:
Such perfect joy therein I find
That it excels all other bliss
That God or nature hath assigned.
Though much I want, that most would have,
Yet still my mind forbids to crave.*

More than one stanza need not be quoted from a composition, already well-known to lovers of our literature, while there are so many which have escaped notice till the present date.

Here is something more original and fanciful, also extracted from one of Byrd's books, 1611:

*In crystal towers and turrets richly set
With glittering gems that shine against the sun,
In regal rooms of jasper and of jet,
Content of mind not always likes to won;
But oftentimes it pleaseth her to stay
In simple cotes enclosed with walls of clay.*

The following in like manner distinguishes itself from the common run of such compositions. It occurs in John Mundy's *Songs and Psalms*, 1594:

*Were I a king, I might command content;
Were I obscure, unknown should be my cares;
And were I dead, no thoughts should me torment,
Nor words, nor wrongs, nor cares, nor hopes, nor fears:
A doubtful choice, of three things one to crave—
A kingdom, or a cottage, or a grave.*

Thomas Campion, with his religious and philosophical soul, was abundant in such strains of poetry. I will select one little piece, which illustrates the loose but genial manner of translation common at that time. It is modelled upon Horace, and has generally been ascribed, but without sufficient reason, as I think, to Lord Bacon:

> *The man of life upright,*
>   *Whose guiltless heart is free*
> *From all dishonest deeds,*
>   *Or thought of vanity.*
>
> *The man whose silent days*
>   *In harmless joys are spent,*
> *Whom hopes cannot delude*
>   *Nor sorrow discontent.*
>
> *That man needs neither towers*
>   *Nor armour for defence,*
> *Nor secret vaults to fly*
>   *From thunder's violence.*
>
> *He only can behold*
>   *With unaffrighted eyes*
> *The horrors of the deep*
>   *And terrors of the skies.*
>
> *Thus scorning all the cares*
>   *That fate or fortune brings,*
> *He makes the heaven his book,*
>   *His wisdom heavenly things.*

> *Good thoughts his only friends,*
>   *His wealth a well-spent age,*
> *The earth his sober inn*
> *And quiet pilgrimage.*

It is now time to embark upon that mighty sea of lyrics which deal with Love and Beauty. The key-note shall be struck by one stanza from a little jewel, set to music by a certain Captain Tobias Hume. The poem itself, like so many of the best in the Greek anthology, is masterless (ἀδέσποτον):

> *O Love, they wrong thee much*
> *That say thy sweet is bitter,*
> *When thy rich fruit is such*
> *As nothing can be sweeter.*
> *Fair house of joy and bliss,*
> *Where truest pleasure is,*
> *I do adore thee;*
> *I know thee what thou art,*
> *I serve thee with my heart,*
> *And fall before thee.*

If that is not the nectar of the gods, distilled in golden numbers, I know not where to find it.

> *Have I found her? O rich finding!*
>   *Goddess-like for to behold;*
> *Her fair tresses seemly binding*
>   *In a chain of pearl and gold.*
> *Chain me, chain me, O most fair,*
> *Chain me to thee with that hair!*

That, too, has no name of author. Yet it is worthy, if not of Shakespeare, at least of the romantic Fletcher. Listen to another, with the dream of music in it. And notice how wonderfully the soul is tuned beforehand to its wavering melodies by the first line, parent of the poem, and parent doubtless of the air:

> *Give beauty all her right!*
>   *She's not to one form tied;*
> *Each shape yields fair delight,*
>   *Where her perfections bide:*
> *Helen, I grant, might pleasing be,*
> *And Ros'mond was as sweet as she.*
>
> *Some the quick eye commends,*
>   *Some swelling lips and red;*
> *Pale looks have many friends,*
>   *Through sacred sweetness bred:*
> *Meadows have flowers that pleasures move,*
> *Though roses are the flowers of love.*
>
> *Free beauty is not bound*
>   *To one unmovèd clime;*
> *She visits every ground,*
>   *And favours every time.*
> *Let the old lords with mine compare;*
> *My sovereign is as sweet and fair.*

Something in the careless touch upon the verse, and something in the metaphysical turn of thought, betrays the authorship of Campion. A rare poet indeed would Campion have been, had not the music satisfied his sense of art in places where the verbal melody runs shallow. Here is a snatch of old song, also by Campion, in one of his best moments; an echo from Catullus:

> *My sweetest Lesbia, let us live and love;*
> *And though the sager sort our deeds reprove,*
> *Let us not weigh them. Heaven's great lamps do dive*
> *Into their west, and straight again revive;*
> *But soon as once is set our little light,*
> *Then must we sleep one ever-during night.*

A lover says this to his lady:

> *Love not me for comely grace,*
> *For my pleasing eye or face,*
> *Nor for any outward part:*
> *No, nor for a constant heart!*
> *For these may fail or turn to ill:*
>   *So thou and I shall sever.*
> *Keep therefore a true woman's eye,*
> *And love me still, but know not why:*
> *So hast thou the same reason still*
>   *To dote upon me ever.*

In the next song, one of Thomas Campion's, we can hear the lilt of the music sounding in its rhythm:

> *Kind are her answers,*
> *But her performance keeps no day;*
> *Breaks time, as dancers,*
> *From their own music when they stray.*

*All her free favours and smooth words
Wing my hopes in vain.
O, did ever voice so sweet but only feign?
Can true love yield such delay,
Converting joy to pain.*

Another by Campion, again with its key-note in the leading line, opens thus :

*Shall I come, sweet Love, to thee
  When the evening beams are set?
Shall I not excluded be?
  Will you find no feignèd let?
Let me not, for pity, more
Tell the long hours at your door.*

Here is good advice to ladies :

*Never love unless you can
Bear with all the faults of man:
Men will sometimes jealous be
Though but little cause they see;
And hang the head as discontent,
And speak what straight they will repent.*

*Men that but one saint adore
Make a show of love to more;
Beauty must be scorned in none,
Though but truly served in one:
For what is courtship but disguise?
True hearts may have dissembling eyes.*

> *Men, when their affairs require,*
> *Must awhile themselves retire;*
> *Sometimes hunt and sometimes hawk,*
> *And not ever sit and talk:*
> *If these and such-like you can bear,*
> *Then like, and love, and never fear!*

This, too, as I find, is by Thomas Campion. Indeed I cannot keep my fingers from the ripe clusters of his honeyed songs, which hang like grapes upon the boughs of poetry. It is not that I seek him out; but he is so admirable in his art that the airs which linger in my memory are mostly his. Perhaps another gatherer of fruit from this abundant garden would be attracted by the songs of other singers. Campion has for me particular charm. Listen to this deep harmony of his. It is addressed to some cruel fair one:

> *When thou must home to shades of underground,*
> *And there arrived, a new admirèd guest,*
> *The beauteous spirits do engirt thee round,*
> *White Iope, blithe Helen, and the rest,*
> *To hear the stories of thy finished love*
> *From that smooth tongue whose music hell can move;*
>
> *Then wilt thou speak of banqueting delights,*
> *Of masques and revels which sweet youth did make,*
> *Of tourneys and great challenges of knights,*
> *And all these triumphs for thy beauty's sake:*
> *When thou hast told these honours done to thee,*
> *Then tell, O tell, how thou didst murder me.*

Was ever the entrance of a proud beauty into the myrtle groves of Elysium, and her reception by the fabled dames of Hellas, more delicately imagined ? Was ever a scholar's and a courtier's compliment more subtly turned to love's upbraiding ?

Well, we must leave Campion for a moment. Take one of the unnamed and unremembered poets :

> *We must not part as others do,*
> *With sighs and tears, as we were two:*
> *Though with these outward forms we part,*
> *We keep each other in the heart.*
> *What search hath found a being where*
> *I am not, if that thou be there ?*
>
> *True love hath wings, and can as soon*
> *Survey the world as sun and moon ;*
> *And everywhere our triumphs keep*
> *O'er absence which makes others weep :*
> *By which alone a power is given*
> *To live on earth, as they in heaven.*

The spiritual note in that last couplet reminds me of another love-ditty, again by Campion, which paints love in its most celestial form. A lady refuses her lover upon earth, and refers him to the charity of souls in heaven, where there is neither marrying nor giving in marriage :

So quick, so hot, so mad is thy fond suit,
  So rude, so tedious grown in urging me,
That fain I would with loss make thy tongue mute,
  And yield some little grace to quiet thee:
An hour with thee I care not to converse,
For I would not be counted too perverse.

But roofs too hot would prove for me all fire,
  And hills too high for my unusèd pace;
The grove is charged with thorns and the bold briar;
  Grey snakes the meadows shroud in every place:
A yellow frog, alas! will fright me so
As I should start and tremble as I go.

Since then I can on earth no fit room find,
  In heaven I am resolved with you to meet:
Till then, for hope's sweet sake, rest your tired mind,
  And not so much as see me in the street:
A heavenly meeting one day we shall have,
But never, as you dream, in bed or grave.

John Dowland shall now present us with one of his dreamy melodies in linked sweetness long drawn out:

Weep you no more, sad fountains;
  What need you flow so fast?
Look how the snowy mountains
  Heaven's sun doth gently waste!
But my sun's heavenly eyes
  View not your weeping;
  That now lies sleeping
Softly, now softly lies
      Sleeping.

> *Sleep is a reconciling,*
>   *A rest that peace begets;*
> *Doth not the sun rise smiling,*
>   *When fair at even he sets?*
> *Rest you then, rest, sad eyes!*
>   *Melt not in weeping;*
>   *While she lies sleeping,*
> *Softly, now softly lies*
>   *Sleeping.*

That is delicious in its drowsy way. And so is the next, by Dowland also:

> *Flow not so fast ye fountains:*
> *What needeth all this haste?*
> *Swell not above your mountains,*
> *Nor spend your time in waste.*
>   *Gentle springs, freshly your salt tears*
>   *Must still fall, dropping from their spheres.*
>
> *Weep they apace, whom Reason*
> *Or lingering Time can ease:*
> *My sorrow can no season,*
> *Nor ought besides appease.*
>   *Gentle springs, freshly your salt tears*
>   *Must still fall, dropping from their spheres.*
>
> *Time can abate the terror*
> *Of every common pain:*
> *But common grief is error,*
> *True grief will still remain.*
>   *Gentle springs, freshly your salt tears*
>   *Must still fall, dropping from their spheres.*

Dowland clearly was of the opinion that " mountains " and " fountains," " haste " and " waste," " sleeping " and " weeping," " tears " and " spheres " were good. Indeed, the exquisite and ever fresh use which is made of these hackneyed verse-materials by the old songwriters stirs our wonder. " Cruel " and "jewel," " treasure " and " measure," " fashion " and "passion" recur again and again. We accept the poor rhymes as part of the game, marvelling at the lyrist's inventive skill in setting them. Somehow, while we read, we feel the music between the verses ; and the music justifies the rhymes.

Let us now hear a maiden complaining of man's inconstancy :

> *Go, turn away those cruel eyes,*
> *For they have quite undone me;*
> *They used not so to tyrannize,*
> *When first those glances won me.*
>
> *But 'tis the custom of you men—*
> *False men, thus to deceive us!*
> *To love but till we love again,*
> *And then again to leave us.*
>
> *Go, let alone my heart and me,*
> *Which thou hast thus affrighted!*
> *I did not think I could by thee*
> *Have been so ill requited.*

> *But now I find 'tis I must prove*
> *That men have no compassion;*
> *When we are won, you never love*
> *Poor women, but for fashion.*
>
> *Do recompense my love with hate,*
> *And kill my heart! I'm sure*
> *Thou'lt one day say, when 'tis too late,*
> *Thou never hadst a truer.*

The man's tone, under similar circumstances, is lighter, as the following ditty shows, one stanza of which I will quote, because of its fanciful refrain:

> *While that the sun with his beams hot*
> *Scorchèd the fruits in vale and mountain,*
> *Philon, the shepherd, late forgot,*
> *Sitting beside a crystal fountain,*
> *In shadow of a green oak tree,*
> *Upon his pipe this song played he:*
> *Adieu, love! adieu, love! untrue love!*
> *Untrue love! untrue love! adieu love!*
> *Your mind is light, soon lost for new love.*

I mentioned Robert Jones as one of those poets whose verses have a certain individuality. The following is a fair specimen of his style:

> *How many new years have grown old*
> *Since first your servant old was new!*
> *How many long hours have I told*
> *Since first my love was vowed to you!*
> *And yet, alas! she doth not know*
> *Whether her servant love or no.*

How many walls as white as snow,
And windows clear as any glass,
Have I conjured to tell you so,
Which faithfully performèd was!
And yet you'll swear you do not know
Whether your servant love or no.

How often hath my pale lean face,
With true characters of my love,
Petitionèd to you for grace,
Whom neither sighs nor tears can move!
O cruel, yet do you not know
Whether your servant love or no.

And wanting oft a better token,
I have been fain to send my heart,
Which now your cold disdain hath broken,
Nor can you heal't by any art :
O look upon't, and you shall know
Whether your servant love or no.

The fluency of this poet, combined with a certain substance of thought, may be exemplified by the following stanza :

Thine eyes, that some as stars esteem,
From whence themselves, they say, take light,
Like to the foolish fire I deem
That leads men to their death by night;
Thy words and oaths are light as wind,
And yet far lighter is thy mind;
Thy friendship is a broken reed
That fails thy friend in greatest need.

Robert Jones, however, when compared with Campion and certain other lyrists, was but a journeyman in verse. This airy little waif of anonymous melody has more the ring of sterling poetry than his lengthy and pretentious compositions :

> *Farewell, my love, I go,*
> *If Fate will have it so !*
> *Yet, to content us both,*
> *Return again as doth*
> > *The bee unto the flower,*
> > > *The cattle to the brook,*
> > *The shadow to the hour,*
> > > *The fish unto the hook,*
> *That we may sport our fill*
> *And love continue still.*

And how metaphysical, how quaint, how fine is this of Campion ! It seems to be an answer to Shakespeare's " Tell me where is fancy bred " :

> *Are you what your fair looks express ?*
> > *O then be kind !*
> *From law of nature they digress*
> > *Whose form suits not their mind :*
> *Fairness seen in th' outward shape*
> *Is but th' inward beauty's ape.*

> *Eyes that of earth are mortal made,*
> > *What can they view ?*

> All's but a colour or a shade,
>   And neither always true:
> Reason's sight, that is etern,
> E'en the substance can discern.
>
> Soul is the Man: for who will so
>   The body name?
> And to that power all grace we owe,
>   That decks our living frame.
> What or how had housen bin
> But for them that dwell therein?
>
> Love in the bosom is begot,
>   Not in the eyes;
> No beauty makes the eye more hot,
>   Her flames the sprite surprise:
> Let our loving minds then meet,
> For pure meetings are most sweet.

How grave and earnest are Campion's admonitions to a Cherubino of the period!

> Thou joyest, fond boy, to be by many loved,
> To have thy beauty of most dames approved;
> For this dost thou thy native worth disguise,
> And playest the sycophant t'observe their eyes:
> Thy glass thou counsell'st, more to adorn thy skin,
> That first should school thee to be fair within.
>
> 'Tis childish to be caught with pearl or amber,
> And womanlike too much to cloy the chamber;
> Youths should the fields affect, heat their rough steeds,
> Their hardened nerves to fit for better deeds:
> Is't not more joy strongholds to force with swords
> Than women's weakness take with looks or words?

*Men that do noble things all purchase glory,
One man for one brave act hath proved a story;
But if that one ten thousand dames o'ercame,
Who would record it, if not to his shame?
'Tis far more conquest with one to live true
Than every hour to triumph lord of new.*

It is hard to believe that the man who composed those serious lines, wrote also the following piece of exquisite light fancy:

*I care not for these ladies
  That must be woo'd and pray'd,
Give me kind Amaryllis,
  The wanton country maid:
Nature art disdaineth,
Her beauty is her own:
    Her when we court and kiss:
    She cries "Forsooth, let go!"
    But when we come where comfort is,
    She never will say "No."*

*If I love Amaryllis,
  She gives me fruit and flowers;
But if we love these ladies,
  We must give golden showers.
Give them gold that sell love,
Give me the nut-brown lass,
    Who when we court and kiss,
    She cries "Forsooth, let go!"
    But when we come where comfort is,
    She never will say "No."*

> *These ladies must have pillows*
> *And beds by strangers wrought;*
> *Give me a bower of willows,*
> *Of moss and leaves unbought:*
> *And fresh Amaryllis,*
> *With milk and honey fed,*
> *Who when we court and kiss,*
> *She cries "Forsooth, let go!"*
> *But when we come where comfort is,*
> *She never will say "No."*

John Dowland's descant upon constancy in love yields one stanza, worthy to rank with Campion's in his philosophic mood:

> *Nature two eyes hath given,*
> *All beauty to impart*
> *As well in earth as heaven,*
> *But she hath given one heart;*
> *That though we see*
> *Ten thousand beauties, yet in us One should be,*
> *One steadfast love,*
> *Because our hearts stand fixt although our eyes*
> *do move.*

Once more I must return to my beloved master Campion. With what serene and simple lucidity the thought flows, and how pleasantly the cadence falls in these two stanzas:

> *When to her lute Corinna sings,*
> *Her voice revives the leaden strings,*
> *And doth in highest notes appear*
> *As any challenged echo clear:*

> *But when she doth of mourning speak,*
> *E'en with her sighs the strings do break.*
>
> *And as her lute doth live or die,*
> *Led by her passion, so must I:*
> *For when of pleasure she doth sing,*
> *My thoughts enjoy a sudden spring;*
> *But if she doth of sorrow speak,*
> *E'en from my heart the strings do break.*

Hardly less beautiful in the same limpid measure are the following lines by an anonymous writer:

> *Dear, do not your fair beauty wrong*
> *In thinking still you are too young;*
> *The rose and lily in your cheek*
> *Flourish, and no more ripening seek;*
> *Inflaming beams shot from your eye*
> *Do show Love's Midsummer is nigh;*
> *Your cherry lip, red, soft, and sweet,*
> *Proclaims such fruit for taste is meet;*
> *Love is still young, a buxom boy,*
> *And younglings are allowed to toy:*
> *Then lose no time, for love hath wings,*
> *And flies away from aged things.*

Before quitting the Elysium of lovers, I shall indulge myself in one more quotation. This shall be a dialogue between a lover and his mistress, composed by some unknown versifier. The swain speaks in the first stanza, praying the maiden of his heart to come forth from her chamber and walk the meadows with him. She replies in the second, giving good reasons for staying at home:

> *Open the door! Who's there within?*
> *The fairest of thy mother's kin!*
> *O come, come, come abroad*
> *And hear the shrill birds sing,*
> *The air with tunes that load!*
> *It is too soon to go to rest,*
> *The sun not midway yet to west:*
> *The day doth miss thee*
> *And will not part until it kiss thee.*
>
> *Were I as fair as you pretend,*
> *Yet to an unknown seld-seen friend*
> *I dare not ope the door:*
> *To hear the sweet birds sing*
> *Oft proves a dangerous thing.*
> *The sun may run his wonted race*
> *And yet not gaze on my poor face,*
> *The day may miss me:*
> *Therefore depart, you shall not kiss me.*

So far as the lyrics from the song-books are known to me, there is nothing gross or licentious in them; even those translated from Italian sources have been bettered in tone by the process, losing something of their sensuous languor, assuming something of that fresh ethereal air which is a peculiar beauty of English poetry in the Elizabethan period.

I pass now to miscellaneous lyrics, some of which take a humorous turn, while others trench upon the ballad. Here is a quaint sort of fable, extracted from Weelkes' Madrigals, 1600:

> *A sparrow-hawk proud did hold in wicked jail*
> *Music's sweet chorister, the nightingale,*
> *To whom with sighs she said: "O set me free!*
> *And in my song I'll praise no bird but thee."*
> *The hawk replied, "I will not lose my diet*
> *To let a thousand such enjoy their quiet."*

The next catch, in which an owl is addressed, has something of the same quaintness; though why owls should be localized in Suffolk, I cannot say. It comes from Vautor's *Songs of divers Airs and Natures*, 1600:

> *Sweet Suffolk owl, so trimly dight*
> *With feathers like a lady bright,*
> *Thou sing'st alone, sitting by night,*
>   *Te whit, te whoo!*
>
> *Thy note, that forth so freely rolls,*
> *With shrill command the mouse controls,*
> *And sings a dirge for dying souls,*
>   *Te whit, te whoo!*

There is a charming little poem in which one girl bids her sister wake at dawn, inviting her to wander forth into the park beneath their window. We owe this to Bateson's *First set of English Madrigals*, 1604:

> *Sister, awake! close not your eyes!*
> *The day her light discloses,*
> *And the bright morning doth arise*
> *Out of her bed of roses.*
>
> *See, the clear sun, the world's bright eye,*
> *In at our window peeping:*
> *Lo! how he blusheth to espy*
> *Us idle wenches sleeping.*
>
> *Therefore, awake! make haste, I say,*
> *And let us, without staying,*
> *All in our gowns of green so gay*
> *Into the park a-maying.*

What a dewy morning-freshness greets us in these careless stanzas; how prettily the ruddy dawn is turned into conceits of roses and of blushes. The style is so simple, the feeling so spontaneous, that we pardon those innocent *concetti*. And the last line carries with it a waft from the burden of a greater poet's masterpiece:

> *Come, my Corinna, come, let's go a-maying.*

Ravenscroft's *Melismata* and *Deuteromelia* deal with a different class of airs from those which have hitherto delayed us. It is in these collections that we find the pathetic old ballad of the Three Ravens, with the melody which Jenny Lind made famous by her thrilling voice and fine dramatic declamation some five-and-twenty years ago. Here too is the catch of the three sailors:

We be three poor mariners.

"A wooing song of a Yeoman of Kent's Son" is another anonymous ditty borrowed from *Melismata:*

> *I have house and land in Kent,*
>   *And if you love me, love me now;*
> *Twopence-halfpenny is my rent,*
>   *I cannot come every day to woo.*
> *(Chorus) Twopence-halfpenny is his rent,*
>   *And he cannot come every day to woo.*

This humorous song, extending to many stanzas, still survives upon the lips of our rustic population. You may hear it, with local variations, at merry-makings in Somersetshire.

One word in conclusion. The songs we have read together are unequal in artistic merit. Some few of them may be valued as flawless gems; and these will pass, I doubt not, into the Golden Treasuries of English lyric poetry. An attentive ear, however, catches many defective accents, halting cadences, slovenly and careless rhymes, prosaic phrases breaking disagreeably on the rhythm. We have to remember that they were made for the singing voice and viol. The unheard melodies of that old music ought to sound in our brain while reading them. I do not say this by way of excuse or apology. I only wish to indicate the way in which they should be taken. Their charm of unaffected grace, their beauty and fragrance as of wilding flowers, remain precious gifts. Few poets, alas! in this age, are natural enough to "recapture that first fine careless rapture," which was as native to the lyrists of the sixteenth century as to thrush or linnet.